The U.S. Supreme Court

"Congress shall make no law . . . abridging the freedom of speech, or of the press."

First Amendment to the U.S. Constitution

The basic foundation of our democracy is the First Amendment guarantee of freedom of expression. The Opposing Viewpoints Series is dedicated to the concept of this basic freedom and the idea that it is more important to practice it than to enshrine it.

OPPOSING
VIEWPOINTS®
SERIES

The U.S. Supreme Court

Other Books of Related Interest:

Opposing Viewpoints Series

Criminal Justice

At Issue Series

Should Cameras Be Allowed in Courtrooms?

Current Controversies Series

Capital Punishment

OPPOSING
VIEWPOINTS®
SERIES

The U.S. Supreme Court

Margaret Haerens, Book Editor

GREENHAVEN PRESS
A part of Gale, Cengage Learning

GALE
CENGAGE Learning™

Detroit • New York • San Francisco • New Haven, Conn • Waterville, Maine • London

Christine Nasso, *Publisher*
Elizabeth Des Chenes, *Managing Editor*

For more information, contact:
Greenhaven Press
27500 Drake Rd.
Farmington Hills, MI 48331-3535
Or you can visit our Internet site at gale.cengage.com

For product information and technology assistance, contact us at

Gale Customer Support, 1-800-877-4253
For permission to use material from this text or product, submit all requests online at www.cengage.com/permissions

Further permissions questions can be emailed to permissionrequest@cengage.com

Articles in Greenhaven Press anthologies are often edited for length to meet page requirements. In addition, original titles of these works are changed to clearly present the main thesis and to explicitly indicate the author's opinion. Every effort is made to ensure that Greenhaven Press accurately reflects the original intent of the authors. Every effort has been made to trace the owners of copyrighted material.

Cover Image copyright © Jose Fuste Raga/Corbis.

LIBRARY OF CONGRESS CATALOGING-IN-PUBLICATION DATA

The U.S. Supreme Court / Margaret Haerens, book editor.
   p. cm. -- (Opposing viewpoints)
   Includes bibliographical references and index.
   ISBN 978-0-7377-4544-3 (hardcover)
   ISBN 978-0-7377-4545-0 (pbk.)
   1. United States. Supreme Court. 2. Political questions and judicial power-- United States. 3. United States. Supreme Court--Officials and employees-- Selection and appointment. 4. Judges--Selection and appointment--United States. 5. Judicial process--United States. 6. Church and state--United States. 7. Constitutional law--United States--Philosophy. I. Haerens, Margaret. II. Title: United States Supreme Court.
  KF8742.U18 2009
  347.73'26--dc22

                            2009025868

Contents

Chapter 4: What Should Be the Judicial Philosophy of the U.S. Supreme Court?

Why Consider Opposing Viewpoints?

> *"The only way in which a human being can make some approach to knowing the whole of a subject is by hearing what can be said about it by persons of every variety of opinion and studying all modes in which it can be looked at by every character of mind. No wise man ever acquired his wisdom in any mode but this."*
>
> John Stuart Mill

In our media-intensive culture it is not difficult to find differing opinions. Thousands of newspapers and magazines and dozens of radio and television talk shows resound with differing points of view. The difficulty lies in deciding which opinion to agree with and which "experts" seem the most credible. The more inundated we become with differing opinions and claims, the more essential it is to hone critical reading and thinking skills to evaluate these ideas. Opposing Viewpoints books address this problem directly by presenting stimulating debates that can be used to enhance and teach these skills. The varied opinions contained in each book examine many different aspects of a single issue. While examining these conveniently edited opposing views, readers can develop critical thinking skills such as the ability to compare and contrast authors' credibility, facts, argumentation styles, use of persuasive techniques, and other stylistic tools. In short, the Opposing Viewpoints Series is an ideal way to attain the higher-level thinking and reading skills so essential in a culture of diverse and contradictory opinions.

In addition to providing a tool for critical thinking, Opposing Viewpoints books challenge readers to question their own strongly held opinions and assumptions. Most people form their opinions on the basis of upbringing, peer pressure, and personal, cultural, or professional bias. By reading carefully balanced opposing views, readers must directly confront new ideas as well as the opinions of those with whom they disagree. This is not to simplistically argue that everyone who reads opposing views will—or should—change his or her opinion. Instead, the series enhances readers' understanding of their own views by encouraging confrontation with opposing ideas. Careful examination of others' views can lead to the readers' understanding of the logical inconsistencies in their own opinions, perspective on why they hold an opinion, and the consideration of the possibility that their opinion requires further evaluation.

Evaluating Other Opinions

To ensure that this type of examination occurs, Opposing Viewpoints books present all types of opinions. Prominent spokespeople on different sides of each issue as well as well-known professionals from many disciplines challenge the reader. An additional goal of the series is to provide a forum for other, less known, or even unpopular viewpoints. The opinion of an ordinary person who has had to make the decision to cut off life support from a terminally ill relative, for example, may be just as valuable and provide just as much insight as a medical ethicist's professional opinion. The editors have two additional purposes in including these less known views. One, the editors encourage readers to respect others' opinions—even when not enhanced by professional credibility. It is only by reading or listening to and objectively evaluating others' ideas that one can determine whether they are worthy of consideration. Two, the inclusion of such viewpoints encourages the important critical thinking skill of objectively evaluating an author's credentials and bias. This evaluation will illuminate an author's reasons for taking a particular stance on an issue and will aid in readers' evaluation of the author's ideas.

It is our hope that these books will give readers a deeper understanding of the issues debated and an appreciation of the complexity of even seemingly simple issues when good and honest people disagree. This awareness is particularly important in a democratic society such as ours in which people enter into public debate to determine the common good. Those with whom one disagrees should not be regarded as enemies but rather as people whose views deserve careful examination and may shed light on one's own.

Thomas Jefferson once said that "difference of opinion leads to inquiry, and inquiry to truth." Jefferson, a broadly educated man, argued that "if a nation expects to be ignorant and free . . . it expects what never was and never will be." As individuals and as a nation, it is imperative that we consider the opinions of others and examine them with skill and discernment. The Opposing Viewpoints Series is intended to help readers achieve this goal.

David L. Bender and Bruno Leone,
Founders

Introduction

> *"The Supreme Court's only armor is the cloak of public trust; its sole ammunition, the collective hopes of our society."*
> —*Irving R. Kaufman*

After the terrorist attacks on New York City and Washington, D.C., on September 11, 2001, the United States immediately began to plan an aggressive campaign to capture or kill the leaders and members of al Qaeda and the Taliban—a campaign that became known as the war on terror. On September 20, 2001, during a televised address to a joint session of Congress, President George W. Bush launched this campaign when he said, "Our war on terror begins with al Qaeda, but it does not end there. It will not end until every terrorist group of global reach has been found, stopped, and defeated." One of the contentious issues that emerged from this war is how the United States should treat terrorism suspects, also known as "enemy combatants."

According to the U.S. Department of Defense, "enemy combatant" is defined as "any person in an armed conflict who could be properly detained under the laws and customs of war." On November 13, 2001, President Bush issued a presidential military commission order that broadened the designation of enemy combatant to refer to an alleged member of the Taliban or al Qaeda. The Bush administration maintained that enemy combatants do not qualify for prisoner-of-war status under the Geneva Conventions and therefore were not entitled to access to the U.S. judicial system and the right of habeas corpus, which is the right to challenge one's detention in court. Essentially, the Bush administration held that it was imperative for U.S. national security to detain Taliban and al

Qaeda suspects indefinitely without charges and to keep suspected terrorists behind bars while active combat operations continued and to ensure suspects could be fully interrogated.

The constitutionality of the Bush administration's treatment of enemy combatants was immediately challenged in court. In 2004, the U.S. Supreme Court heard the case of suspected Taliban fighter Yaser Esam Hamdi, a U.S. citizen who was being held as an enemy combatant after being captured in Afghanistan in 2001. Hamdi argued that as a U.S. citizen he was entitled to the right of habeas corpus. The Supreme Court decided in favor of that argument, effectively curtailing the power of the U.S. government to indefinitely imprison U.S. citizens without allowing them their right of habeas corpus. In fact, eight of the nine justices of the Court concurred in *Hamdi v. Rumsfeld* that the president does not hold the authority to detain a U.S. citizen without basic due process protections enforceable through judicial review.

Also in 2004 the Court ruled on *Rasul v. Bush*, a key case that held that the U.S. court system has the authority to decide whether foreign nationals held in the U.S. prison at Guantanamo Bay Naval Base in Cuba were wrongfully imprisoned. After being captured as a suspected terrorist in Afghanistan, Shafiq Rasul was subsequently designated as an enemy combatant at Guantanamo Bay, which meant he did not have access to counsel, the right to a trial, or knowledge of the charges against him. He challenged his detention, and the Supreme Court held that the U.S. judicial system had jurisdiction at Guantanamo Bay. The majority of justices decided that foreign nationals being held at Guantanamo could challenge their detentions in U.S. courts. Congress attempted to invalidate this decision with the Detainee Treatment Act in 2005 and the Military Commissions Act in 2006. These acts amended the federal statute to eliminate habeas jurisdiction for enemy combatants held in U.S. custody, creating instead a much more limited review that allowed individuals to challenge only the U.S. government's classification of them as enemy combatants.

In 2006, the Court heard the case of *Hamdan v. Rumsfeld.* In this case, Salim Ahmed Hamdan, a citizen of Yemen and suspected terrorist, was captured in Afghanistan and subsequently imprisoned at Guantanamo Bay. In 2004, he was charged with conspiracy to commit terrorism and was scheduled to go on trial before a military commission authorized under the military commission order of 2001. Hamdan's lawyers filed a petition for a writ of habeas corpus, claiming that it was illegal to try him in front of a military commission because such a procedure lacked the protections required under the Geneva Conventions and the U.S. Uniform Code of Military Justice. The Supreme Court ruled in favor of Hamdan's argument, holding that the military commissions at Guantanamo Bay were in direct violation of Common Article 3 of the Geneva Conventions. The Court also held that the president was not authorized to set up military commissions like the ones at Guantanamo; congressional authority is needed for such a step.

On June 12, 2008, the Supreme Court issued a historic decision in another landmark case regarding the U.S. treatment of enemy combatants, *Boumediene v. Bush.* In its ruling, the Court struck down the part of the Military Commissions Act of 2006 that sought to deny federal habeas corpus jurisdiction over enemy combatants detained at Guantanamo Bay. The Court held that the act violated the Suspension Clause of the U.S. Constitution and Guantanamo Bay detainees have a constitutional right to file petitions for habeas corpus in U.S. federal courts, challenging the lawfulness of their detention.

In these four landmark cases, the Supreme Court made key rulings on issues such as the jurisdiction of the U.S. judicial system, the power of the executive branch in wartime, and the right of habeas corpus for U.S. citizens and foreign nationals. Many critics of these rulings argue that the Supreme Court should not limit presidential powers. These critics believe it is the president, and not the courts, who should be making decisions on how to treat detainees and prosecute suspected terrorists. Supporters of the Supreme Court decisions maintain the role of the Court is performing its constitutional duties by acting as a check on the executive branch.

The authors of the viewpoints presented in *Opposing Viewpoints: The U.S. Supreme Court* explore many of the challenges facing the Court in the following chapters: What Should Be the Role of the U.S. Supreme Court? How Should the U.S. Supreme Court Rule on Moral and Religious Issues? What Factors Should Be Considered for U.S. Supreme Court Nominees? What Should Be the Judicial Philosophy of the U.S. Supreme Court? The information provided in this volume will provide insight into the debate over the role of the Court as it faces myriad ongoing controversies and new challenges.

OPPOSING
VIEWPOINTS®
SERIES

CHAPTER 1

What Should Be the Role of the U.S. Supreme Court?

Chapter Preface

Established by the Judiciary Act of 1789, the U.S. Supreme Court first assembled on February 1, 1790. The authority of the Court was established by Article III of the U.S. Constitution, which held that "The judicial power of the United States, shall be vested in one Supreme Court, and in such inferior courts as the Congress may from time to time ordain and establish." However, the Constitution did not spell out the specific powers, duties, or obligations of the Court. Instead, it left it up to the Congress and Supreme Court justices themselves to determine the authority and precise operations of the Court.

Under Chief Justice John Marshall, the Supreme Court made great strides in defining its power with a landmark 1803 decision in *Marbury v. Madison*. In this case, the Court established its power to interpret the U.S. Constitution and to decide the constitutionality of laws passed by Congress and the state legislatures. As the Court began acting as a strong check on both the executive and legislative branches of government—it generated a long-standing debate about its proper role within the three branches of government. This debate continues today.

In one sense, the Supreme Court has carved out significant power. It makes the final decision on all cases involving the U.S. Constitution and the laws passed by Congress. It can determine whether a president's actions are unconstitutional. It can resolve that laws passed by Congress violate the U.S. Constitution and nullify those laws. It can also rule that a state government has passed a law that is unconstitutional.

However, there are also significant limits on the power of the U.S. Supreme Court. The other two branches of government—the executive and legislative branches—can impose these limitations. For example, the president nominates justices to the Court, and the U.S. Senate must confirm the nomination after substantial debate and hearings. In this way, the president and Senate have a huge influence on the judicial philosophy and political ideology of potential Supreme Court justices. The Court can be swayed by political movements and trends.

The viewpoints in the following chapter explore the role of the Supreme Court. They discuss whether the Court should be viewed as an independent and impartial arbiter or if it should be more reflective of the dominant political ideology of the era. Also examined in this chapter is the role of the Court in determining the fate of enemy combatants held by the United States, how far the Court should go in checking the powers of the executive branch, and whether the Court should be more aggressive in preempting state laws in its decisions.

"The [U.S. Supreme Court] justices used the [recent terrorism] cases to wrestle with one of the core dilemmas of a free society: How can strength be balanced with liberty? Or, put another way, what are the limits on a leader's power in a crisis?"

The U.S. Supreme Court Can Be a Check on the Executive Branch

David von Drehle

David von Drehle is a Washington Post *staff writer. In the following essay, von Drehle interprets three recent U.S. Supreme Court decisions on terrorism cases—whether foreign prisoners may use U.S. courts to challenge their imprisonment, determining whether a U.S. citizen could be held as an "enemy combatant" without a hearing, and a challenge to the status of accused terrorist and U.S. citizen Jose Padilla—as a check on executive powers.*

As you read, consider the following questions:

1. According to the author, what was Justice Sandra Day O'Connor's concern about the indefinite detention of terrorist suspects?

2. What precedents does von Drehle say the U.S. Supreme Court justices drew from when forming their own opinions?

3. Why were some justices dissatisfied with the outcomes, according to the author?

The Supreme Court's complicated holdings in three cases involving detainees from the battle against terrorism may not result in any prisoners going free—the justices yesterday [June 28, 2004] left that for lower courts or tribunals to decide.

But the opinions, concurrences and dissents were decisive on this: They represent a nearly unanimous repudiation of the Bush administration's sweeping claims to power over those captives.

Justices Agree To Check Executive Power

Liberal or conservative mattered little in the ultimate outcome. The court roundly rejected the president's assertion that, in time of war, he can order the "potentially indefinite detention of individuals who claim to be wholly innocent of wrongdoing," to quote the court's opinion in the case of foreign prisoners held at the U.S. base in Guantanamo Bay, Cuba. In fact, the administration's claim to such power over U.S. citizens produced an opinion signed by perhaps the court's most conservative justice, Antonin Scalia, and possibly its most liberal, John Paul Stevens.

Expansion of Powers

It's not shocking that the Bush administration sought to expand its powers. It's shocking that the president unfailingly refuses to ask.

There are two explanations for the Bush administration's failure to stay within the boundaries of the legal structures for which it's bargained: One is that the administration believes it is fighting this war on its own; the courts, the Congress, and the American people are all standing in its way. The other is that the administration is convinced that none of our statutes or policies or systems will actually work in a pinch. Our laws aren't just broken. They are unfixable.

Dahlia Lithwick,
"Uncivil Liberties," Slate.com,
December 21, 2005.

"The very core of liberty secured by our Anglo-Saxon system of separated powers has been freedom from indefinite imprisonment at the will of the Executive," Scalia wrote, with Stevens's support.

In this way, the court's rejection of the executive-power arguments in the cases might be seen as part of a reemergence of the other branches of government from the shadow of the Sept. 11, 2001, terrorist attacks. As the justices suggested several times in their opinions, emergency measures that might have been within the president's power in the days and weeks just after 9/11 now must be reconciled with American norms of due process. In that sense, the cases struck a chord with congressional hearings into the rules for prisoner interrogations at U.S. prisons in Iraq and Afghanistan.

Due Process Is a Fundamental Principle

Given that the administration has said its war on terrorism might stretch over generations, Justice Sandra Day O'Connor wrote, the "indefinite detention" of a prisoner "could last for the rest of his life." And that, the court said, is too long to do without the basics of due process.

Only Justice Clarence Thomas embraced the administration's positions without reservation, referring in a dissenting opinion to "the breadth of the President's authority to detain enemy combatants, an authority that includes making virtually conclusive factual findings" that the Supreme Court is powerless to "second-guess."

Each case before the court presented slightly different facts—there was a case asking whether foreign prisoners captured in the terrorism war had a right in U.S. courts to challenge their imprisonment, a case asking whether a U.S. citizen could be held as an "enemy combatant" without a hearing of some kind, and a case challenging the short-circuiting of a criminal case against accused terrorist Jose Padilla, a U.S. citizen, by placing him in military custody as an enemy combatant.

But the justices used the cases to wrestle with one of the core dilemmas of a free society: How can strength be balanced with liberty? Or put another way, what are the limits on a leader's power in a crisis?

"The defining characteristic of American constitutional government is its constant tension between security and liberty," Justice David H. Souter wrote.

And so the opinions drew heavily on some of the oldest and weightiest precedents in the book. Starting with King John's promise in the Magna Carta, signed in 1215, that "no free man should be imprisoned . . . save by the judgment of his peers or by the law of the land," the justices traced the limits on executive power through English common law, on through the Federalist Papers and down a long line of precedents forged in some of the darkest hours of the nation, including the Civil War and World War II.

"We have long since made clear that a state of war is not a blank check for the President when it comes to the rights of the Nation's citizens," O'Connor wrote in a painstakingly nuanced opinion ordering a hearing for U.S. citizen Yaser Esam Hamdi, who was taken captive in Afghanistan.

The Future Is Unclear

The justices left unresolved exactly how tightly they intend to try to rein in the president. All of them paid deference to the heavy responsibility of the commander in chief and his duty to keep the country secure. Even as they reaffirmed the bedrock principle of checks and balances, they left [George W.] Bush and his successors substantial room to operate.

They admonished lower courts to tread carefully on national security matters. They resolved the Padilla case—which could have been the most provocative—on narrow jurisdictional grounds. And they stopped far short of ruling that citizens who are designated enemy combatants must be charged as criminals and given the full access to the courts that would entail.

This moderation ultimately left the court's liberal wing unsatisfied. Stevens, joined by Justices Souter, Ruth Bader Ginsburg and Stephen G. Breyer, argued passionately that the Padilla case should have been dealt with head on. "At stake in this case is nothing less than the essence of a free society. . . . Unconstrained Executive detention for the purpose of investigating and preventing subversive activity is the hallmark of the Star Chamber [a British court for which the monarchy appointed judges and was controversial due to secret proceedings and lack of trial by jury of peers]," he wrote.

Yet if, in the end, the justices could not agree on exactly how far the president can go, they were clear that he had already gone too far.

> "American history is rife with executives stretching national security threats in order to enhance their political power and the only branch of government that has the institutional power to constrain them is Congress."

The U.S. Supreme Court Is Not an Effective Check on the Executive Branch

Lisa L. Miller

Lisa L. Miller is an Assistant Professor of Political Science at Rutgers University in New Jersey and a contributor to Foreign Policy in Focus, a foreign policy think tank in Washington, D.C. In the following essay, she argues that the U.S. Supreme Court has not historically been a strong check on the executive branch. Instead, Congress has been the only branch that has consistently limited the power of the presidency and should continue to do so when warranted.

As you read, consider the following questions:

1. Why does the author believe that Alexander Hamilton referred to the judiciary as "the least dangerous branch" of government?

2. How did the U.S. Supreme Court rule in the infamous case, *Korematsu v. U.S.?*

3. What does the author perceive as the "single most important lesson" of Supreme Court history on cases regarding executive power?

Under the [George W.] Bush administration, foreign policy issues such as warrantless wiretaps, the rights of enemy combatants, and interrogation methods have become the latest topics in the longstanding debate over the limits of executive branch power and the role of the judiciary in enforcing those limits. The issue recently took center stage when Senate Democrats expressed concern at the confirmation hearings of Samuel Alito, President Bush's most recent [2005] pick for the Supreme Court, that Alito would support greater judicial deference to executive authority.

In Federalist #78, Alexander Hamilton referred to the judiciary as "the least dangerous branch" of government. This was true, Hamilton reasoned, because the judiciary had neither "force nor will." Since Congress held the power of the purse, and the executive the power of the sword, the judicial branch of government was in the weakest position to threaten the interests of citizens.

In the more than 200 years since Hamilton made his case, the federal judiciary has grown in size and scope and is often regarded as serving a crucial function as the stopgap on excessive legislative and executive power. Many citizens look back over the 20th century and see the Supreme Court championing individual freedoms and standing in the way of government abuse of power. Indeed, when I teach Constitutional Law, I am always struck by the degree of confidence students place in Supreme Court decisions as though they are self-executing, self-enforcing, and provide some mystical transformation of political interaction. Left-leaning students in particular seem to assume that the Supreme Court has rallied behind progressive causes and reined in executive and legislative power.

A Modest Role for the Supreme Court

The actual role of the Supreme Court in American history is more modest and its decisions are as likely to reinforce excessive acts of legislative and executive power as to challenge them. As it turns out, Hamilton's assumptions are quite accurate. The Supreme Court must rely on the other branches of government to enforce its decisions and as an unelected body that must react to cases brought before it, the Court is highly constrained in the issues it can address. A brief look at cases involving executive power reveals few instances in which the court bucked the status quo. The best we can say about Supreme Court rulings in this area is that they have, on occasion, drawn some loose boundaries around presidential authority. However, in the absence of clear congressional opposition to executive action, the Supreme Court has largely affirmed broad discretion, particularly in times of war or other national security crises. This is not surprising since the Constitution provides specific powers to both Congress and the executive in these areas but grants no such direct authority to the Supreme Court.

In one of its most famous and notorious sanctions of executive power, *Korematsu v. U.S.* (1941), the Supreme Court refused to hold unconstitutional President [Franklin D.] Roosevelt's Executive Order interning Japanese citizens. While this case has been roundly criticized by citizens and government officials alike, the Supreme Court has never overturned the precedent or the presumption that wartime expands executive authority. Even a case widely recognized for imposing limitations on executive power, *Youngstown Sheet and Tube v. Sawyer* (1952), does little to draw clear boundaries in the absence of congressional disapproval. The decision, which involved President [Harry S.] Truman's seizure of privately owned steel mills to keep labor disputes from disrupting steel production during the Korean War, struck down Truman's actions as a violation of the president's constitutional authority. However, in that case, Congress had specifically considered and rejected providing the president with this method of resolving labor disputes. The decision, then, can be seen as much as a reaffirmation of congressional decision-making as an example of the Supreme Court's willingness to rein in exuberant executives. The court explicitly acknowledged that executive power is at its lowest ebb when it acts contrary to congressional intent and without clear constitutional authorization. But this leaves the field wide open because Congress often provides authorization for executives to act in the interest of national security and because presidents have long laid claim to inherent powers in matters of foreign policy and national security. In fact, in *United States v. Curtiss-Wright Corp.* (1936), the Supreme Court went out of its way to declare that the president has broader authority when he acts in foreign matters than in domestic ones.

Some see the court's ruling in *Hamdi v. Rumsfeld* (2004) as a sincere curtailment of executive power because eight of nine justices refused to acquiesce to the Bush administration's claim that Congress' Authorization to Use Military Force in Afghanistan allowed the president to detain an American citizen indefinitely on little more than its own say-so. But, writing for the majority, Sandra Day O'Conner actually reaffirmed the broad power of the executive branch to detain citizens, even indefinitely, when Congress has authorized discretion as it did in Afghanistan and Iraq. The court's decision did hold the government to a higher standard by refusing to accept the administration's argument that a flimsy affidavit by one executive agent was sufficient to justify the detention, and by requiring the government to allow Hamdi to challenge that detention. But the thrust of the majority and concurring

> ## Congress' Check on Executive Powers Has Decreased
>
> For decades, imperatives of wars hot and cold, and the sprawl of the regulatory state, have enlarged the executive branch at the expense of the legislative. For eight years, the Bush administration's "presidentialists" have aggressively wielded the concept of the "unitary executive"— the theory that where the Constitution vests power in the executive, especially power over foreign affairs and war, the president is immune to legislative abridgements of his autonomy.
>
> George F. Will, *"Making Congress Moot,"*
> Washington Post, *December 21, 2008.*

opinions were consistent with the court's previous decisions on executive power, which indicate deference to Congress and an unwillingness to shorten the presidential tether in the absence of congressional intent to the contrary.

A Deferential Judiciary

In fact, this is probably the single most important lesson of Supreme Court history on cases involving executive power. *Where Congress has provided even modest enabling legislation or has simply refused to act contrary to the executive, the Supreme Court has rarely stepped into the breach.* We return again to Hamilton. With no enforcement power or constitutional mandate to address national security concerns, the Supreme Court is generally reluctant to substitute its judgment for that of legislators. In the absence of egregious and obvious abuse of power, it is largely deferential to the branches of government that have access to intelligence information that guides decision-making. Of course, there is a long history of this information being distorted (U.S.S. Maine, Gulf of Tonkin) but it is hard to see how the Supreme Court is better situated to ferret out these distortions than Congress.

The recent appointment of Samuel Alito to replace Sandra Day O'Conner generated concern among Democrats that his view of executive power is too broad. But given the court's history, it seems unlikely to make a substantial difference. A few cases might turn out to favor the president by a 5-4 vote but few presidents, least of all this one [George W. Bush], would appoint someone who is openly hostile to executive power. Any decision favoring the president then, is less likely to be a function of Samuel Alito on the bench than of the fact that the Democrats do not control Congress or the presidency. It is worth noting here that the only member of the court whose opinion in *Hamdi* would satisfy the most ardent resisters of executive power was Antonin Scalia (appointed by President Reagan), who wrote that in the absence of a suspension of habeas corpus by Congress, the executive has only two choices for American citizens: charge them with a crime or let them go.

James Madison wrote that "war is the true nurse of executive aggrandizement" as he made the case for legislative control over the war-making machinery of government. "Hence, it has grown into an axiom," Madison continued, "that the executive is the department of power most distinguished by its propensity to war: hence it is the practice of all states, in proportion as they are free, to disarm this propensity and its influence." It would have been inconceivable to Madison to rely on the anemic judicial branch of government to do this disarming. Only the branch empowered directly by the consent of the people and with all of the law-making and fiscal power behind it, can serve as a counterweight to the siren call of war that seems to be heard by all executives.

American history is rife with executives stretching national security threats in order to enhance their political power and the only branch of government that has the institutional power to constrain them is Congress. Reliance on the Supreme Court is not only likely to disappoint, it is also foolhardy for it permits Congress to abdicate the genuinely revolutionary role given to it by the Framers which allows the use of the full military might of the United States government only with the active consent of the governed. Democrats in Congress who look to a Republican president to appoint a Supreme Court justice willing to buck tradition and limit executive power in any substantial way are barking up the wrong tree. If executives are to be reined in, Congress is going to have to get off its duff and fulfill its constitutional mandate all on its own.

> *"As critically important as the Boume-diene decision is for the place of law in the war on terror ..., its most profound implications may lie in what it reflects about altered conceptions of sovereignty, territoriality, and rights in the globalized world."*

The U.S. Supreme Court Should Decide the Rights of Enemy Combatants

David D. Cole

David D. Cole is a professor at Georgetown University Law Center in Washington, D.C. In the following essay, he assesses the significance of the U.S. Supreme Court's Boumediene v. Bush *decision, which declared "enemy combatants"—those accused of working with the enemy in an armed conflict—have a constitutional right to challenge the legality of their detention in federal court. Cole argues that giving enemy prisoners the right to habeas corpus, which allows them to challenge their detention before a judge, is fundamental to the protection of all other rights.*

David D. Cole, "Rights over Borders," *Cato Institute Supreme Court Review*, 2007–2008, pp. 47–52. Copyright © 2007–2008 CATO Institute. Republished with permission of CATO Institute, conveyed through Copyright Clearance Center, Inc.

Cole asserts that the Court's decision is consistent with a transnational trend to give greater prominence to human rights in matters of national security.

As you read, consider the following questions:

1. According to the author, what is the first way in which the *Boumediene* decision is groundbreaking?

2. According to Cole, to whom does the *Boumediene* decision extend the constitutional right of habeas corpus?

3. Which courts around the world does Cole cite as issuing major decisions that favored individual rights over political rights on questions of terrorism and national security?

In June 2008, more than six years after the first prisoners were brought to a makeshift military prison camp at Guantanamo Bay, Cuba—bound, gagged, blindfolded, and labeled "the worst of the worst"—the Supreme Court in *Boumediene v. Bush* declared that they have a constitutional right to challenge the legality of their detention in federal court. The detainees may be excused if they did not leap for joy at the result. After all, the Court ordered no one released, did not address the question of whether the detainees were lawfully detained or treated, and merely decided as a threshold matter that they had a right to take their cases to a federal district court—a question the Court seemed to have decided four years earlier in the first Guantanamo case it considered, *Rasul v. Bush*. Yet the decision was in fact a profound—and in many respects surprising—defeat for the [George W.] Bush administration in the legal "war on terror." It means that Guantanamo is no longer a "law-free zone"—and that the courts will play a vital role in ensuring that the rule of law applies to the ongoing struggle with Al Qaeda. As critically important as the *Boumediene* decision is for the place of law in the war on terror, however, its most profound implications may lie in what it reflects about altered conceptions of sovereignty, territoriality and rights in the globalized world.

Three Ways *Boumediene* Is Groundbreaking

Boumediene is groundbreaking in at least three respects. First, for the first time in its history, the Supreme Court declared unconstitutional a law enacted by Congress and signed by the president on an issue of military policy in a time of armed conflict. While the Court has on rare occasions found that presidents exceeded their powers where they acted *contrary* to congressional will during wartime, as in *Youngstown Sheet & Tube Co. v. Sawyer* and *Little v. Barreme*, this decision went much further, upending the joint decision of the political branches acting together on a military matter during a time of military conflict.

Second, and also for the first time, the Court extended constitutional protections to noncitizens outside U.S. territory during wartime. As recently as 2001, the Court had stated—without reasoning—that the Constitution was no solace for foreign nationals outside our borders, articulating a traditional understanding of the Constitution as guided by territory and citizenship. Yet in *Boumediene* the Court extended the constitutional right of habeas corpus not only to foreign nationals outside our borders, but to what some might call the modern-day equivalent of "enemy aliens"—foreign nationals said to be associated with the enemy in wartime.

Third, the Court declared unconstitutional a law restricting federal court jurisdiction. The Court has traditionally sought to avoid such confrontations through the application of statutory interpretation, bending over backward to interpret statutes to preserve judicial review where it might be unconstitutional to deny such review. Only on two prior occasions has the Court actually declared a jurisdiction-stripping law unconstitutional, and on both occasions it found reasons for doing so that were independent of the pure question of jurisdiction. The courts have traditionally avoided enforcing constitutional limits on Congress's control over jurisdiction because congressional control is seen as important in conferring democratic legitimacy on an unelected institution. Yet in *Boumediene*, despite the availability of statutory constructions that could have saved the statute, the Court declared Congress's repeal of habeas corpus unconstitutional.

Critics Object to Decision

The result in *Boumediene* was also surprising because the government had precedent on its side. In 1950, the Supreme Court had expressly ruled that the writ of habeas corpus was unavailable to enemy fighters captured and detained abroad during wartime. Both the district court and the court of appeals had found that decision, *Johnson v. Eisentrager*, to be controlling, and no subsequent case law had directly undermined its reasoning.

Critics will point to these features as evidence that the Court's decision was illegitimately "activist." To many observers, there are good reasons for judicial reticence in military matters, especially where the political branches act in concert; good reasons not to extend constitutional protections to foreign nationals; and good reasons for the Court to avoid a direct confrontation with Congress over the scope of its jurisdiction. Justice Antonin Scalia charged in dissent that "[w]hat drives today's decision is neither the meaning of the Suspension Clause, nor the principles of our precedents, but rather an inflated notion of judicial supremacy."

At the same time, the decision was not entirely unprecedented. It vindicated the right to a "writ of habeas corpus," an ancient form of judicial remedy that finds its origins in the Magna Carta, and that the Framers deemed so fundamental that they included it in the main body of the Constitution at a time when they considered a "Bill of Rights" unnecessary. Habeas corpus gives prisoners the right to challenge the legal-

---

Justice Anthony Kennedy's Opinion

In his majority opinion [for *Boumediene v. Bush*], Associate Justice Anthony Kennedy wrote, "Within the Constitution's separation-of-powers structure, few exercises of judicial power are as legitimate or as necessary as the responsibility to hear challenges to the authority of the executive to imprison a person. . . . Liberty and security can be reconciled; and in our system they are reconciled within the framework of the law."

"Landmark Win for Guantanamo Detainees!"
Center for Constitutional Rights, *2008.*

---

ity of their detentions in court, and is both an essential part of the separation of powers and the "stable bulwark of our liberties." It is fundamental to the protection of all other rights, because no right can be safely exercised if the government is free to imprison people without judicial recourse.

In addition to enforcing a fundamental and long-standing right, the Court applied established doctrine—albeit in a new setting. In assessing whether the constitutional right of habeas corpus extended to Guantanamo, the Court applied a contextual and pragmatic inquiry that it had developed and applied in assessing whether constitutional rights extend to "unincorporated territories," jurisdictions over which the United States exercises control but does not intend to incorporate as states. That test asks whether the application of a given constitutional right would be "anomalous or impracticable" in light of the particular circumstances of the jurisdiction, and applies those rights that would not create serious anomalies or impracticalities.

Assessing the Decision

The real significance of the Court's decision in *Boumediene*, however, lies not in whether it correctly applied or modified past precedent to a novel context, but in what it portends for modern-day conceptions of sovereignty, territoriality, and rights. For all its assertions that "everything changed" after the terrorist attacks of September 11, the Bush administration relied on old-fashioned conceptions of sovereignty and rights in arguing that habeas corpus jurisdiction did not extend to Guantanamo, and that federal courts should have no constitutionally recognized role there. The Court's decision, by contrast, reflects new understandings of these traditional conceptions, understandings that pierce the veil of sovereignty, reject formalist fictions of territoriality where the state exercises authority beyond its borders, and insist on the need for judicial review to safeguard the human rights of citizens and noncitizens alike.

While *Boumediene* may appear unprecedented from a domestic standpoint, it fits quite comfortably within an important transnational trend of recent years, in which courts of last resort have played an increasingly aggressive role in reviewing (and invalidating) security measures that trench on individual rights. The Law Lords in Britain, the Supreme Courts of Canada and Israel, the European Court of Human Rights, and the Constitutional Court of Germany have all issued major decisions restricting political prerogative on issues of terrorism and national security in the name of individual rights.

The Impact of Globalization

These increasingly confident judicial assertions of authority in turn reflect global transformations in international law since the end of World War II, including most significantly international human rights law. The latter half of the 20th century and the beginning of the 21st have witnessed an extraordinary explosion of human rights, beginning with the UN's [United Nations'] Universal Declaration of Human Rights, and finding reflection in international treaties such as the International Covenant on Civil and Political Rights, the Geneva Conventions, and the Convention Against Torture. This trend is reinforced by regional agreements for the establishment and enforcement of human rights, especially the European Convention on Human Rights; the growth in influence and power of nongovernmental human rights groups; the increasing resort by domestic courts to international and comparative standards in the interpretation of their own laws; and the recognition of "universal jurisdiction" as a way of holding abusers of certain fundamental human rights accountable wherever they are found.

These developments have transformed international law from a subject that concerned only state-to-state relations to one that focuses just as significantly on the relations of states to their own citizens, and to others subject to their authority. In particular, international human rights law has made substantial inroads on traditional notions of sovereignty and territoriality that once left states both unaccountable to outsiders for what they did to their own citizens inside their borders, and unaccountable to domestic law for what they did to others outside their borders. The lasting significance of *Boumediene* will rest on its recognition of, and critical role in, the transformation of our understandings of this interplay between sovereignty, territoriality, and human rights.

> "The ingrained bias against the elected
> branches and their ability to make well-
> reasoned and just judgments is destruc-
> tive to the entire notion of representa-
> tive government."

The Fate of Enemy
Combatants Is Not a Matter
for Judicial Review

Mark R. Levin

*Mark R. Levin is a conservative political commentator, radio
host, and author. In the following viewpoint, he argues that the
Constitution gives primacy over war-related matters to the president, not the U.S. Supreme Court. He finds, therefore, it is not
the judiciary's role to make decisions about national security
matters, particularly the rights of enemy combatants during
wartime.*

As you read, consider the following questions:

1. What was the ruling by the U.S. Supreme Court in the
   Rasul v. Bush case?

2. Why does the author believe an earlier Supreme Court ruling—*Johnson v. Eisentrager*—should have resulted in a much different outcome in the *Rasul* case?

3. What did Justice Antonin Scalia outline as the implications of the *Rasul* decision, according to the author?

Nothing in the Constitution gives parity, much less primacy, to the courts over war-related matters. Indeed, as Thomas argues, the Constitution assigns such authority to the president. The Supreme Court somehow believes that courts are more qualified or trustworthy to rule on detentions. But why is that? Why is it assumed that judges are more competent in weighing the rights of individuals against national-security needs? The ingrained bias against the elected branches and their ability to make well-reasoned and just judgments is destructive to the entire notion of representative government. If elected officials cannot be trusted to make wise decisions about national security, then they cannot be trusted to make decisions at all. There is no evidence that the president has abused his constitutional authority in detaining Hamdi or anyone else. There has been no widespread detention of U.S. citizens—only two, to the best of my knowledge—and only after an extensive vetting process. This hardly justifies the Court's intervention and usurpation of executive authority.

The issues in *Hamdi* do not present garden-variety criminal matters, yet the Supreme Court couldn't resist treating Hamdi's detention this way by cobbling together an unclear due-process requirement, which will be left to the lower courts to figure out.

These days, a single U.S. citizen working in collaboration with al Qaeda or other terrorist groups is potentially more dangerous to more people in this nation than any foreign standing army. And information he might have about future attacks—combined with the government's need for secrecy to thwart them—justifies a decision by the president to detain "illegal combatants" without judicial second-guessing.

As bad as the *Hamdi* decision was, the Supreme Court went even further in *Rasul v. Bush*. In *Rasul*, the Court determined that federal courts could hear cases in which *foreign* enemy combatants challenge their detention. *Rasul* involved two Australian citizens and twelve Kuwaiti citizens "who were captured abroad during hostilities between the United States and the Taliban."

These enemy combatants have also been detained at Guantanamo Bay. Justice John Paul Stevens, writing for the majority, ruled that they had the right to petition the federal courts to review their status as detainees. Stevens devoted considerable verbiage attempting to distinguish the facts in *Rasul* from the 1950 Supreme Court opinion in *Johnson v. Eisentrager*. *Eisentrager* established the principle that aliens detained outside the sovereign territory of the United States could not ask federal courts to review their status. The reasoning of the Court was explained by Robert D. Alt, a fellow in legal and international affairs at the John Ashbrook Center for Public Affairs:

> [Proceedings by alien detainees] would hamper the war effort and bring aid and comfort to the enemy. They would diminish the prestige of our commanders, not only with enemies but with wavering neutrals. It would be difficult to devise more effective fettering of a field commander than to allow the very enemies he is ordered to reduce to submission to call him to account in his own civil courts and divert his efforts and attention from the military offensive abroad to the legal defensive at home. Nor is it unlikely that the result of such enemy litigiousness would be [a] conflict between judicial and military opinion highly comforting to enemies of the United States.

In *Eisentrager*, twenty-one German nationals were taken into custody in China at the conclusion of World War II. They were tried and convicted of war crimes by a U.S. military tribunal in China. They were then remitted to a military prison in Germany. These individuals sought to bring their case to America by filing a writ of habeas corpus in the U.S. District Court for the District of Columbia. The issue was whether alien combatants should have access to civilian courts.

Justice Robert Jackson, writing for the Supreme Court's majority, was adamant in denying aliens this access: "We are cited to no instance where a court in this or any other country where the writ [of habeas corpus] is known, has issued it on behalf of an alien enemy who, at no relevant time and in no stage of his captivity, has been within its territorial jurisdiction."

Jackson realized the danger enemy combatants posed. "But these prisoners were actual enemies, active in the hostile service of an enemy power. There is no fiction about their enmity." The German soldiers were denied the ability to petition civilian courts for review of their status.

War limits the right of certain aliens to access U.S. courts, or at least it used to. As Jackson wrote:

It is war that exposes the relative vulnerability of the alien's status. The security and protection enjoyed while the nation of his allegiance remain in amity with the United States are greatly impaired when his nation takes up arms against us. While his lot is far more humane and endurable than the experience of our citizens in some enemy lands, it is still not a happy one. But disabilities this country lays upon the alien who becomes also an enemy are imposed temporarily as an incident of war and not as an incident of alienage.

Obviously, we are not at war with the home countries of the individuals who initiated the *Rasul* case (they are citizens of Australia and Kuwait). However, the principle is the same. When these men joined the Taliban and fought for al Qaeda, they became part of an organization that is at war with the

United States. Denying foreign enemy combatants access to U.S. courts is an "incident of war."

Eisentrager was clear. The enemy combatants in *Rasul* should never have been granted the right to challenge their detentions in federal courts. Stevens dismantled the precedent established in *Eisentrager*, claiming that the facts in *Rasul* were sufficiently different to compel a contrary result:

> Petitioners [in *Rasul*] differ from the *Eisentrager* detainees in important respects: They are not nationals of countries at war with the United States, and they deny that they have engaged in or plotted acts of aggression against the United States; they have never been afforded access to any tribunal, much less charged with and convicted of wrongdoing; and for more than two years they have been imprisoned in territory over which the United States exercised exclusive jurisdiction and control.

The fact is that *Eisentrager* and *Rasul* are identical in two significant respects—both involved foreign enemy combatants who never set foot in America, and both involved the detention of foreign enemy combatants outside the United States. There was no reason for the Court to take up this case, and no reason to reverse *Eisentrager*. Stevens and the majority were bent on substituting their preferred view for the president's.

Stevens also attempted to distinguish *Eisentrager* by relying on a statute, which states, in part: "Writs of habeas corpus may be granted by the Supreme Court, any justice thereof, the district courts and any circuit judge *within their respective jurisdiction*." (Emphasis added.)

This, too, is disingenuous. Stevens decided that "within their respective jurisdiction" means any territory over which the United States exercises complete control, but not "ultimate sovereignty," such as on a military base located in a foreign country. Clearly, however, "within their respective jurisdiction" means the territorial locations that demarcate each federal

What Is an "Enemy Combatant"?

An "enemy combatant" is an individual who, under the laws and customs of war, may be detained for the duration of an armed conflict. In the current conflict with al Qaida and the Taliban, the term includes a member, agent, or associate of al Qaida or the Taliban. In applying this definition, the United States government has acted consistently with the observation of the Supreme Court of the United States in Ex parte Quirin, 317 U.S. 1, 37–38 (1942): "Citizens who associate themselves with the military arm of the enemy government, and with its aid, guidance and direction enter this country bent on hostile acts are enemy belligerents within the meaning of the Hague Convention and the law of war."

William Haynes, "Enemy Combatants,"
Council on Foreign Relations, December 12, 2002.

court's reach. Guantanamo Bay is outside such locations; consequently, the law has no application. No matter. Here is how Stevens rewrote the statute: "[B]ecause the writ of habeas corpus does not act upon the prisoner who seeks relief, but upon the person who holds him in what is alleged to be unlawful custody, a district court acts within [its] respective jurisdiction within the meaning [of the law] as long as the custodian can be reached by service of process."

Any enemy combatant can now challenge his detention in a federal court provided the combatant (or the combatant's relatives or friends) is able to deliver a lawsuit to the Department of Defense or the Department of Justice.

The practical implications of this decision are immense. As Justice Antonin Scalia explained:

The consequence of this holding, as applied to aliens outside the country, is breathtaking. It permits an alien captured in a foreign theater of active combat to [bring a suit] against the Secretary of Defense. Over the course of the last century, the United States has held millions of alien prisoners abroad. A great many of these prisoners would no doubt have complained about the circumstances of their capture and the terms of their confinement. The military is currently detaining over 600 prisoners at Guantanamo Bay alone; each detainee undoubtedly has complaints—real or contrived—about those terms and circumstances. The Court's unheralded expansion of federal-court jurisdiction is not even mitigated by a comforting assurance that the legion of ensuing claims will be easily resolved on the merits. . . . From this point forward, federal courts will entertain petitions from these prisoners, and others like them around the world, challenging actions and events far away, and forcing the courts to oversee one aspect of the Executive's conduct of a foreign war.

Former federal prosecutor Andrew C. McCarthy made an excellent point when he wrote:

[W]hen our military fighting overseas, at the height of active hostilities, grants quarter by apprehending rather than destroying the forces arrayed against it, those forces, those alien enemies trying to kill Americans—alien enemies who secrete themselves among civilians; who use humanitarian infrastructure like ambulances, hospitals and schools to carry out their grisly business; who make a mockery of the laws and conventions of civilized warfare; who torture and kill their captives with a bestiality that defies description; whose only contact with America is to regard her with this savagery—have resort to the courts of the United States to protest their detention and to compel the executive branch, while it is conducting battle, to explain itself. Just to describe this breathtaking claim of entitlement should be to refute it. Yet the United States Supreme Court has ruled in favor of the enemy.

So now, for the first time in American history, captured alien enemy combatants will have access to our courts. They will be afforded some kind of due process hearing and one day I expect they'll have a right to competent counsel, paid for by the American taxpayer, and the right to compel testimony from the soldiers who apprehended them. Even for the Supreme Court, this is a grotesque perversion of the Constitution.

In truth, despite allegations of vast civil liberties violations, President Bush has conducted this war with great restraint, when compared with the actions of past presidents. For example, Article I of the Constitution describes the legislative powers of Congress. Among those powers, Section 9, Clause 2 provides that, "The Privilege of the Writ of Habeas Corpus shall not be suspended, unless when in Cases of Rebellion or Invasion the public Safety may require it." Yet, on several occasions during the Civil War, President Abraham Lincoln suspended the writ to silence or punish those who were sympathetic to slavery or states' rights. As author Craig Smith describes:

During the Civil War, President Lincoln suspended the writ of habeas corpus first in Maryland and then in southern Ohio because of its sympathy for slavery and states' rights and its geographic location. Reluctantly, Lincoln took the action against Maryland so that he could prevent its legislature from meeting and voting for secession. In September of 1861, nine members of the Maryland legislature were arrested. It was the first time a president of the United States had prevented a state legislature from meeting and was a clear violation of their constitutional rights. However, the threat of Civil War was so severe that Lincoln felt justified in his unprecedented action.

The same would be true in Ohio. During his campaign for governor of Ohio, Congressman Clement L. Vallandigham gave a fiery speech in southern Ohio in support of the rebel effort. When General Burnside read reports of the speech in the newspaper, he had Vallandigham arrested and sent to Boston for trial. Lincoln eventually exiled the Congressman to the South because he had some doubts about incarcerating a sitting congressman for delivering a political campaign speech.

Lincoln's suspension of the writ of habeas corpus was eventually challenged by John Merryman, a secessionist and citizen of Maryland. The case reached the Supreme Court, where the chief justice was Roger B. Taney (author of the 1857 *Dred Scott* decision upholding slavery). In *Ex parte Merryman*, Taney, writing for the Court, held that only Congress could suspend the writ of habeas corpus. Lincoln ignored the opinion. In 1863, Congress passed a statute authorizing Lincoln to suspend the writ.

Obviously, President Bush hasn't imprisoned or exiled members of Congress or state legislators who oppose his handling of the war on terrorism. Indeed, he hasn't taken any actions to silence his critics. The Bush administration has detained only two U.S. citizens, and then only for overt acts of war.

On February 19, 1942, during World War II, President Franklin Roosevelt issued Executive Order 9066, which directed military commanders to designate areas "from which any or all persons may be excluded." While the order didn't apply specifically to a particular ethnic group, its effect was clear. Tens of thousands of Japanese Americans and Americans of Japanese ancestry were systematically removed from their homes in western coastal regions and forced into internment camps—not because of any evidence of criminal or disloyal behavior, but because of their race.

The president has not issued an edict rounding up, say, law-abiding Islamic and Arab Americans, or Americans of Arab ancestry, forcing them into guarded camps where the government could watch over them. In fact, the administration is loath to give special scrutiny to aliens who travel to the United States even from countries known to harbor or tolerate terrorists, including the home countries of the September 11, 2001, terrorists. For the Supreme Court to intervene in the *Hamdi* and *Rasul* cases, and use them as vehicles to usurp the commander in chief's role despite the president's restraint, is indefensible as a matter of law and policy. Thanks to the Supreme Court's ruling, in July 2004, the detainees at Guantanamo Bay were informed they could use American courts "to contest their detention."

It is difficult to win a war when the enemy is armed not only with rifles and rocket propelled grenades, but also with subpoenas, affidavits, and lawyers. And it's difficult to maintain a republic when the judiciary abuses its constitutional authority. These cases illustrate perhaps more than any others just how dangerous and reckless an unbridled judiciary can be, not only to the Constitution, but to our national security.

"[The] politicization of the Supreme Court by President [George W.] Bush is dangerous to the rule of law and precedent, equal rights before the law, and our nation's democratic principles."

Some Conservative Justices Have Violated the Rule of Law for Political Reasons

Center for American Progress

The Center for American Progress (CAP) is a liberal think tank and advocacy organization. In the following viewpoint, the center asserts that President George W. Bush appointed partisan appointees in John Roberts and Samuel Alito, two conservative judges who have tilted the Supreme Court to the right. The center provides examples to prove how both Roberts and Alito have undermined the rule of law in order to reach conservative political decisions.

As you read, consider the following questions:

1. How did President George W. Bush describe John Roberts and Samuel Alito when he nominated them?

2. According to CAP, how did Roberts and Alito describe their judicial positions before being nominated?

3. What are the three ways CAP believes Roberts and Alito have violated the rule of law?

At the outset of the still-unfolding scandal over the firing of nine United States Attorneys and the politicization of the hiring process at the Department of Justice [DOJ], Attorney General Alberto Gonzales was adamant that he would "never, ever" replace a United States attorney for political reasons. Deputy Attorney General Paul McNulty called the allegation of politicization at the DOJ "like a knife to my heart." Now we know that political officials at DOJ "crossed the line" many times in an effort to place "loyal Bushies" in positions of power.

Unfortunately, a similar story appears to be unfolding at the Supreme Court. When introducing John Roberts and Samuel Alito, President Bush argued that Roberts and Alito deserved bipartisan support because they would "interpret the Constitution and the laws faithfully and fairly, to protect the constitutional rights of all Americans," and they would not "impose their preferences or priorities on the people." The nominees similarly promised to be "umpires" without "any agenda" or "any preferred outcome in any particular case."

These statements at the time seemed hard to reconcile with facts in the record. On the campaign trail, President Bush had rallied his base with promises to nominate "strict constructionists" to the Supreme Court in the mold of Antonin Scalia and Clarence Thomas. Roberts, meanwhile, had been part of what his former colleague Bruce Fein called a "band of ideological brothers" who argued for dramatic changes in the law during the Reagan administration. Alito had submitted a 1985 job application detailing his "disagreement with Warren Court opinions" and his desire to "help advance legal positions [of the Reagan administration] in which

I personally believe very strongly." Indeed, both Roberts and Alito spent their early careers serving the executive branch of ideologically driven administrations rather than gaining the kind of real world experience brought to the Court by justices such as the one Alito replaced, Sandra Day O'Connor.

The Senate and the American people by and large believed the promises made by Bush, Roberts, and Alito and discounted the discordant facts in the record. Both judges were confirmed with bipartisan support. One Senator, before voting for the confirmation of Chief Justice Roberts, said: "Today I will vote my hopes and not my fears."

Sadly, after nearly two terms together on the Supreme Court, it is clear that the Senate's fears about Roberts and Alito are being realized, their hopes dashed. Last term, Roberts and Alito voted together in 88 percent of non-unanimous cases—more than any other two justices. So far this term, Roberts and Alito have voted together in 18 of the 20 cases that have divided the Court by five to four margins. Together with Justices Thomas and Scalia, Alito and Roberts have formed a solid conservative bloc of four justices in every major case, splitting the court along ideological lines.

In reaching a conservative political outcome in these cases, Justices Roberts and Alito have run roughshod over many of the critical rule of law principles that limit the role politics can play in judicial decision-making, including respect for equal access to the courts, respect for the democratic process, and respect for precedent.

The Supreme Court's brace of rulings today are thoroughly emblematic of the two justices' disrespect for all three legal principles. In *Leegin Creative Leather Products v. PSKS*, Roberts and Alito voted to overturn a nearly century-old decision preventing manufacturers from setting a minimum price retailers may charge for their products.

The decision by Alito and Roberts to overturn this long-established precedent is particularly remarkable because the case involves interpretation of a statute. The Court is particularly committed to *stare decisis* in statutory cases because Congress can amend a statute if it thinks the Court has erred in its interpretation. This disregard for precedent may be a historic first. Breyer asserts in dissent: "I am not aware of any case in which this Court has overturned so well-established a statutory precedent."

Chief Justice Roberts's opinion, joined by Alito in the Louisville [Kentucky] and Seattle race cases—*Parents Involved in Community Schools v. Seattle School District No. 1* and *Meredith v. Jefferson County Board of Education*—so perfectly illustrates the rule-of-law concerns raised by this term's opinion that it warrants its own discussion.

As an initial matter, the opinion vividly contradicts Roberts's professed preference for crafting "narrow" opinions that achieve as much consensus as possible on the Court. There were five votes on the Court for the proposition that the Seattle and Louisville plans did not meet the Court's strict scrutiny test for race-conscious classifications. Roberts's opinion could have ended with this conclusion.

Instead, Roberts wrote two additional sections, joined only by Alito, Scalia, and Thomas, which fully equate race-conscious efforts to promote integration with racial segregation and root this conclusion in the Supreme Court's landmark ruling in *Brown v. Board of Education*. There is, in Stevens's words, a "cruel irony" in this use of the *Brown* opinion, and these deeply divisive conclusions were totally unnecessary for the resolution of the case.

As Kennedy argues quite forcefully in a separate opinion, Roberts "is too dismissive of the legitimate interests government has in ensuring all people have equal opportunity regardless of their race." This is just one of many rule-of-law concerns highlighted by Roberts's opinion in the Seattle and Louisville cases:

• Roberts and Alito show an alarming lack of *respect for precedent*. As Breyer argues persuasively in dissent, Roberts's opinion refuses to follow a "longstanding and unbroken line of legal authority [that] tells us that the Equal Protection Clause permits local school boards to use race-conscious criteria to achieve positive race-related goals, even when the Constitution does not compel it."

• Roberts and Alito fail to *respect the democratic process*. The plurality portions of their opinion, in particular, would overturn decisions made by elected officials in communities across the country. As Breyer puts it in dissent the "Constitution allows democratically elected school boards to make up their own minds as to how best to include people of all races in one America."

• Roberts and Alito *disregard constitutional history*. Some conservatives, notably Scalia and Thomas, purport to be bound by the original understanding of the Constitution. But there is no evidence that anyone alive at the time the 14th Amendment was passed thought it would ban race-conscious efforts to promote integrated schools. Indeed, as Breyer demonstrates, historical research shows that the generation of Americans who enacted the Equal Protection Clause also used race-conscious measures to promote school integration. Roberts's opinion ignores this constitutional history.

The opinions joined by Roberts and Alito are by no means isolated cases. Consider the following:

Respect for Precedent

Following a doctrine known as *stare decisis*, Latin for "let it stand," the Supreme Court generally builds off its prior rulings rather than overruling them. Yet in several recent cases, Alito and Roberts have treated this doctrine, and the Court's earlier rulings, with an alarming lack of respect.

Bowles v. Russell: Alito and Roberts voted to overrule two long-standing Supreme Court rulings even though no one in the case had filed a brief asking the Court to overrule these cases.

Gonzales v. Carhart: Roberts and Alito upheld a federal abortion ban that contains no exception for the health of a woman even though the law was nearly identical to the law *struck down* by the Court only seven years earlier in *Stenberg v. Carhart*. As Justice Ginsburg noted in dissent, the opinion joined by Alito and Roberts "is hardly faithful to our earlier invocations of 'the rule of law' and the 'principles of *stare decisis*.'"

FEC v. Wisconsin Right to Life: Roberts and Alito voted to dramatically curtail restrictions on "sham issue ads," regulated by the Bipartisan Campaign Reform Act. While Roberts and Alito purport not to overrule the Supreme Court's 2003 ruling in *McConnell v. FEC*, the other seven justices all agreed that their opinion "effectively overrules *McConnell* without saying so." In Justice Scalia's words: "[t]his faux judicial restraint is judicial obfuscation."

National Association of Home Builders v. Defenders of Wildlife: Roberts and Alito ruled that Section 7 of the Endangered Species Act, which requires that all federal agencies "shall" insure that their actions do not jeopardize endangered species, does not apply to nondiscretionary federal actions. This ruling contradicts the Court's earlier ruling in *TVA v. Hill*, which explained that Section 7 "admits of no exception." As Justice Stevens notes in dissent, this ruling "turns its back on our decision in *Hill* and places a great number of endangered species in jeopardy."

Hein v. Freedom from Religion: Roberts and Alito threw out a lawsuit challenging President Bush's Faith-Based Initiative ruling that taxpayers had no "standing" to challenge the program, notwithstanding the Court's 1968 ruling in *Flast v. Cohen* that found taxpayer standing in a very similar context.

Number of Conservative Votes on U.S. Supreme Court, 1937–2006

10 "Most Conservative" Justices		10 "Least Conservative" Justices	
Justice Name	Percentage Conservative Votes	Justice Name	Percentage Conservative Votes
Clarence Thomas	.822	Thurgood Marshall	.211
William Rehnquist	.815	William Douglas	.213
Antonin Scalia	.757	Frank Murphy	.241
John Roberts	.753	Wiley Rutledge	.247
Samuel Alito	.740	Arthur Goldberg	.248
Warren Burger	.735	William Brennan	.265
Sandra Day O'Connor	.680	Hugo Black	.283
Lewis Powell	.677	Earl Warren	.308
Charles Whittaker	.673	Ruth Bader Ginsburg	.312
Anthony Kennedy	.647	Benjamin Cardozo	.333

TAKEN FROM: William M. Landes and Richard A. Posner, "Rational Judicial Behavior: A Statistical Study," *Social Science Research Network*, April 2008.

Justice Souter, in dissent, asserts that "a search of [the Alito/Roberts plurality] opinion for a suggestion that these taxpayers have any less stake in the outcome than the taxpayers in *Flast* will come up empty: the plurality makes no such finding, nor could it." Justice Scalia is even more scathing, stating in a concurrence that "laying just claim to be honoring *stare decisis* requires more than beating *Flast* to a pulp and then sending it out to the lower courts weakened, denigrated, more incomprehensible than ever, and yet somehow technically alive."

Respect for the Democratic Process

Absent clear constitutional mandates, unelected judges should generally defer to the decisions on complex policy questions made by Congress—the branch of our federal government most representative of the will of the people. In many cases over the last two terms, Roberts and Alito have voted in ways that show a disturbing lack of deference, if not outright hostility, to the laws passed by Congress.

FEC v. Wisconsin Right to Life: Roberts and Alito effectively overturned the reasoned judgment of a bipartisan majority in Congress that "sham issue ads" were corrupting the nation's political process.

Ledbetter v. Goodyear: Alito and Roberts ignored both the broad remedial mandate of Title VII of the Civil Rights Act of 1964 and the intent of Congress in the Civil Rights Act of 1991 in ruling that a victim of workplace discrimination could not sue her employer even when intentional past discrimination continued to result in current disparities in pay.

Rapanos v. U.S.: Alito and Roberts joined a plurality ruling that sought to dramatically limit the reach of the Clean Water Act, leaving vast amounts of the waters and wetlands currently protected by the Act unprotected. Justice Kennedy described the opinion joined by Alito and Roberts as "unduly dismissive of the interests asserted by the United States in these cases." Justice Stevens was blunter, stating that the opinion joined by Roberts and Alito displayed "antagonism to environmentalism."

Massachusetts v. EPA: Roberts and Alito voted in dissent to deny the EPA authority under the Clean Air Act to address global warming pollution—even though the Act itself called carbon dioxide a pollutant. Justice Stevens, writing for the Court's majority, explained that this interpretation was flatly inconsistent with the text of the Act.

Arlington Cent. Sch. Dist. v. Murphy: Roberts and Alito voted that parents who successfully challenge their local school board for violating the mandates of the Individuals with Disabilities Education Act should not recover the costs of retaining the expert witnesses necessary to prevail in such suits—even though Congress clearly intended that such costs be recoverable.

National Association of Homebuilders v. Defenders of Wildlife: Alito and Roberts refused to follow the clear mandate from Congress that every federal agency should consider the impact of each of its actions on the continued survival of endangered species.

Respect for Equal Access to Courts

Roberts told the Senate that he would be an umpire, just calling balls and strikes. But Alito and Roberts have frequently ruled in ways that have shut the courthouse doors, effectively preventing a game from even beginning. Most disturbingly, court-access rulings by Roberts and Alito seem designed mainly to exclude particular types of litigants, such as victims of discrimination and criminal defendants, who have long been disfavored by political conservatives. These rulings disrespect the edict of the great Chief Justice Marshall in *Marbury v. Madison*, which holds: "[t]he very essence of civil liberty certainly consists in the right of every individual to claim the protection of the laws, whenever he receives an injury. One of the first duties of government is to afford that protection."

Bowles vs. Russell: Roberts and Alito voted to deny an appeal of a district court ruling because the appeal was filed two days late—even though the untimely filing was caused by the erroneous instructions given Bowles in an order issued by a federal district judge.

Schriro v. Landrigan: Alito and Roberts refused to order a hearing on a claim of ineffective assistance of counsel in a death penalty case, finding that the petitioner waived his right to present mitigating evidence. In dissent, Justice Stevens observed that the outcome could "only be explained by [the majority's] increasingly familiar effort to guard the floodgates of litigation." But as Stevens pointedly notes, "doing justice does not always cause the heavens to fall."

Ledbetter v. Goodyear: Alito and Roberts threw out a Title VII suit even though a jury found Ms. Ledbetter was the victim of intentional sex discrimination and that, as a result, she was receiving less money in each paycheck than men in similar positions and with similar seniority. Under the rule they imposed, a victim of discrimination is required to file a complaint even before he or she is aware that a discriminatory decision has been made—or be barred from court forever.

Hein v. Freedom for Religion: Roberts and Alito voted to close the Court's doors on taxpayers arguing that the President's Faith-Based Initiative promoted religious organizations in violation of the Constitution's Establishment Clause.

In short, the Roberts and Alito on the Supreme Court are nothing like the Roberts and Alito in testimony before Congress and public appearances before the American people prior to their confirmation by the Senate to the nation's highest bench. This politicization of the Supreme Court by President Bush is dangerous to the rule of law and precedent, equal rights before the law, and our nation's democratic principles.

"Liberals win victory after victory after victory in the judiciary—advancing a radical agenda that could never win approval in the democratic process."

Liberals Exercise Too Much Control over the U.S. Judiciary

Mark W. Smith

Mark W. Smith is a conservative commentator and author. In the following viewpoint, Smith contends that the U.S. judicial system, including the Supreme Court, has ruled in favor of liberal principles and interests despite conservative political gains. Smith perceives this left-wing dominance in the courts has hurt the United States and urges conservative jurists to abandon judicial restraint and instead practice judicial activism.

As you read, consider the following questions:

1. What successes does the author list as proof of left-wing dominance of the U.S. judicial system?

2. How does the author believe conservatives can "thwart the liberal legal assault"?

Mark W. Smith, *Disrobed*. New York: Crown Publishing Group, 2006. Copyright © 2006 MSMW, LLC. Used by permission of Crown Publishers, a division of Random House, Inc.

3. According to the author, how will conservative judicial activism help conservative causes?

These days conservatives rail against the courts, and with good reason. Liberals win victory after victory after victory in the judiciary—advancing a radical agenda that could never win approval in the democratic process. Consider: Today's law permits the starving of a woman in Florida but not of a dog; permits aborting an unborn child but criminalizes the destruction of spotted-owl eggs; permits the consideration of race in law school admissions but does not allow wardens to consider the racial composition of prison gangs in making decisions about cell assignment; considers minors too immature to be executed for murder but more than capable of deciding whether to have an abortion without consulting parents; grants more legal protection to the "right" to abortion—which is mentioned nowhere in the Constitution—than to the right to property or right to bear arms, both of which are identified in the Constitution; and forbids laws banning virtual child pornography but permits federal laws criminalizing the running of political advertisements in the months leading up to a federal election.

American courts have gone so far as to increase taxes, ban nativity scenes in public parks during Christmas, mandate the approval of gay marriage, declare the recitation of the Pledge of Allegiance in public schools unconstitutional because it contains the phrase "under God," prevent public schools from inviting clergy to give nondenominational prayers at graduation ceremonies, compel states to provide free taxpayer-funded public education to illegal immigrants, restructure election districts, resolve presidential and gubernatorial elections, and second-guess presidential decisions about how to fight a war.

And the Left continues to achieve extraordinary success in the courts even now, despite the sharp right turn the nation has taken over the past quarter century; despite Republican control of the White House, both houses of Congress, and most state legislatures and governorships; despite the fact that Republican presidents have appointed most of America's federal judges; and despite the fact that for the past thirty years at least seven of the nine Supreme Court justices have been Republican appointees—something that should temper the enthusiasm of conservatives who rejoice in the mere ascension of John Roberts and Samuel Alito. Conservatives rightly recognize that what Alexander Hamilton once called the "least dangerous branch" of government has instead become the *most* dangerous branch.

Something Is Wrong

Something is wrong here—something is very wrong.

In the popular Harry Potter books and movies, the game Quidditch revolves around the Golden Snitch—a small, winged ball that zips around the playing field. Basically, when a player captures it, the game ends and his team wins. The courts have become the Golden Snitch of American politics: If one party captures the courts, that team wins. The party then has the ultimate power: to strike down laws that the elected branches enact and to shape American society for decades to come. And the frightening truth is that the Left has held the Golden Snitch for some seventy years, despite the Republicans' success at the polls.

No conservative who is being honest with himself can deny how badly we're getting beaten in the courts. The question, then, is: *Why* do we keep losing? How does the loony Left, discredited virtually everywhere and in countless respects, keep using the legal system to advance its radical social and political agenda seemingly at will? The conservative movement includes many sincere, intelligent, earnest representatives committed to keeping liberal judges from destroying "the land of the free and home of the brave." Yet we've made little progress in our fight to stop the left-wing judicial assault.

I've spent years in the legal and political trenches fighting for the conservative cause—as vice president of the New York City Federalist Society, as a practicing attorney, as an author, and as a legal and political commentator on television and radio. I've worked closely with many of the Right's most able legal and political minds and spoken at length with them about how we can fix this urgent problem. I've attended more law conferences, speeches, and lectures than I care to count in hopes of helping the Right fight back. And I've long wanted to believe that the solutions the conservative movement usually advances would finally begin to pay off, for many of these proposals come from conservatives and legal experts whose opinions I deeply respect. Indeed, for many years and in countless media appearances I have argued passionately for many of these same ideas. But the lessons of history—underscored by the eye-opening Harriet Miers [nominated Oct. 3, 2005, to the Supreme Court by President George W. Bush, but due to opposition from both sides of the political spectrum, her nomination was withdrawn on October 27] experience—have led me to conclude, reluctantly, that a new approach is required.

Conservatives Are Self-Defeating

The plain truth is this: The Right will never thwart the liberal legal assault until we abandon our own self-defeating tactics. That's right, *self-defeating*. Our current strategy (such as it is) is to pillory [to expose to public derision] liberals for their underhanded (albeit highly effective) tactics in the courts—judicial activism, inventing rights and principles found nowhere in the Constitution, ignoring legal precedents when it suits their needs, relying on foreign precedent to justify desired outcomes, suing to achieve in the courts what they can't achieve through the democratic process, and much more. And after we attack, criticize, and harangue the Left, we propose this alternative: *Everyone should play by the rules—the rule of law.*

"More to the Right!" Cartoon by Harley Schwadron. www.CartoonStock.com.

In essence, all that proposal amounts to is this: *Hey, guys, this isn't right. Let's cut it out.*

Yes, that's it. You've heard it all before, though not quite in those terms. Instead, you hear it phrased in terms of the Right's favorite legal catchphrases. Think back to the Supreme Court nominations of John Roberts and Samuel Alito. How many times did you hear Republican politicians and conservative commentators—judges, academics, editorial writers, syndicated columnists, television and radio hosts—call for "judicial restraint," "judges who strictly interpret the law," "judges who won't legislate from the bench," "an end to judicial activism," "judges who respect the rule of law," or some variation thereof?

It all sounds great, and indeed conservatives should be credited for having a clear conception of how the Framers intended the judiciary to work—that judges should *not* be "politicians in black robes" with the power to determine how we all live our lives. In fact, I think we can all agree that it would be ideal if the judiciary really did play the role in society conservatives say it should.

Conservatives Must Change Strategy

But I'm here to tell you: It ain't happening. Yes, I would love to embrace the Constitution and use its text to resolve all questions of constitutional law. I would love it if judges stopped focusing on political outcomes—upholding laws whose objectives they support while striking down laws of which they disapprove. I would love it if courts hadn't spent the past seventy years inventing certain rights and taking others away from Americans. I would love it if left-wing legal organizations stopped filing lawsuit after lawsuit after lawsuit until finally they get the political outcome they want. Like it or not, though, all of these things are realities of twenty-first-century American law and politics. Simply wishing they didn't exist will not make them disappear. Sorry, conservatives, we're not in Kansas anymore.

And even if somehow, magically, we could click our heels and get every one of the thousands of judges in America—many of them proud liberals with lifetime appointments—to stop legislating from the bench, what would that buy us? Not enough, because this step does nothing to address the seventy years of liberal legal precedents now on the books. In essence, the conservative proposal of judicial restraint is purely a defensive measure. It would try to lock in the status quo—and the status quo is a legal system that skews radically to the left. As conservatives, we must finally admit to ourselves that not only is our approach to the courts fanciful, it's not even *desirable*. We can't remain blindly committed to the same losing strategy.

Plan of Action

So what do we do? We must stop playing defense against the courts and instead go on offense by *using* the courts. We must take back the law from liberal judicial activists and thwart the loony Left's assault on America. Fortunately, there's a secret weapon we can use to do that. And the weapon is lying right in front of us, hiding in plain sight, ours for the taking. It's a secret only in the sense that the conservative movement refuses to consider it as an option. In fact, it's a weapon that the Left has wielded against us for decades, and with startling results.

The weapon? Judicial activism.

Yes, judicial activism—the very thing conservatives decry at every turn.

Wait, does this mean I've become a feel-good liberal, torn up my vast-right-wing-conspiracy membership card, turned my back on the Federalist Society, and become Air America's seventy-ninth listener? Not at all. . . . Conservative attacks on judicial activism have missed the point: The problem with the courts is not judicial activism per se, but *liberal* judicial activism. Judicial activism is nothing but a tool; what matters is for what purposes the tool is applied—for good or for bad.

Use Conservative Judicial Activism

Radical as it may sound to conservatives who have been taught that judicial activism is an inherent evil, our secret weapon— *conservative* judicial activism—in fact offers us the greatest opportunity to preserve and protect the rights, freedoms, and ideals that the Constitution was designed to protect and that America's Founders cherished. Even those committed to ending judicial activism altogether must realize this point: No strategy conservatives adopt, other than engaging in judicial activism ourselves, will end judicial activism by the Left.

Conservatives now have a golden opportunity not just to thwart future liberal gains but actually to convert America's courts into allies of the Right and the American way of life. Now is not the time to settle for half measures. Embracing such strategies as "judicial restraint" may have made sense in a previous era when the conservative movement was confined to the margins of American political life, but we are now in a position to start governing, not just reacting to the Left. Times have changed, and the Right's tactics should, too.

| "Our forefathers believed that we all stand equal and have natural rights even before the existence of government."

The U.S. Judiciary Should Be Independent and Impartial

Frederic F. Fleishauer

Frederic F. Fleishauer is a judge with the Portage County Circuit Court in Wisconsin. In the following speech presented at the 2005 Wisconsin Judicial Conference, Fleishauer underscores the importance of an independent and impartial judiciary, tracing the historical basis for the concept and describing the pressure put on judges to rule in political ways.

As you read, consider the following questions:

1. What does the Declaration of Independence say about King George and his judiciary?

2. What were the feelings of James Madison regarding the importance of an independent judiciary, according to the author?

Frederic F. Fleishauer, "Communicating the Value of an Independent Judiciary," *Wisconsin Court System*, May 2005. Reproduced by permission of the author.

3. What does the author list as threats to an independent judiciary?

To communicate the value of something, we must understand it ourselves. A definition and a review of our history lessons will help us start. The definition I like the best may be the least helpful, but it has a good sound bite. The Hon. Michael Kirby, a fellow Justice from the downunder [Australia], in a speech . . . said: "A judge without independence is a charade wrapped inside a farce inside an oppression." Justice Kirby went on: "The alternative to the rule of law is the rule of power, which is typically arbitrary, self-interested and subject to influences which may have nothing to do with the applicable law or the factual merits of the dispute. Without the rule of law and the assurance that comes from independent decision makers, it is obvious that equality before the law will not exist."

Our forefathers believed that we all stand equal and have natural rights even before the existence of government. People establish constitutions to express their rights and create a government subject to them. From the [French Enlightenment] political philosopher [Baron de] Montesquieu then came the concept that separating the powers of government into branches protected these rights of the people. What role did the judiciary play in this plan?

The Founding Fathers Wanted an Impartial Judiciary

The Declaration of Independence listed as one of our grievances that King George III had made judges dependent on his will for the tenure of their offices and their salaries. The drafters of the Constitution well knew that if the legislative or executive [branches] determined the meaning of the laws or Constitution, there would be no independence, only a new form of tyranny. James Madison, drafter of the Bill of Rights, expected the judiciary to resist every encroachment by the legislature or the executive on the rights expressed in the Constitution. He felt only permanent tenure gave the judiciary the necessary independence to complete such an arduous duty. Permanent tenure was so important because courts have no power to do anything on their own. You may have experienced that at one time or another, and Rep. John Hostettler [former U.S. representative from Indiana] felt the need to point it out again recently [in a 2004 speech to the Christian Coalition] when he said, "Federal courts have no army or navy."

So the judiciary standing alone, with no power or purse, no army or navy, received the charge to defend the liberty of the people through protecting the law, the Constitution. In his decision in *Marbury v. Madison*, Chief Justice [Thurgood] Marshall added the final twist to the equation. It held the judiciary had the power of judicial review, the power to judge the constitutionality of the actions of the other branches. It thus placed the judiciary in the center of ongoing political controversies, and often at the focal point of the failures of our society.

Challenges to the Judiciary

The judiciary face all kinds of threats in their task: a hostile majority upset with protection granted a minority; poor communication between branches of government; demands for impeachment for unpopular decisions; unfilled judicial vacancies impacting workload; elections overpowered by the wealthy; appointment of weak, unqualified or corrupt candidates who can't or won't exercise independent judgment; non-payment of salaries; non-payment of the expenses of the court; and political limitations on jurisdiction or the substance of what the courts can consider.

Our Australian friend Kirby finished his definition: "The real test comes when judges are led by their understanding of the law, the findings on the facts and the pull of conscience to a decision which is contrary to what the other branches of government or other powerful interests in society want. Something different from what the home crowd wants." Then you determine what independence of the judiciary means. By the way, by citing foreign authority I've just joined Supreme Court Justice [Anthony] Kennedy on Congress's list of suspect judges.

Reviewing the Record

How has this played out? Historically, we have seen the successes. At the height of World War II, the Court excused Jehovah's Witnesses from the responsibility of the Pledge of Allegiance. After *Brown v. the Board of Education*, efforts to abolish life tenure on the Supreme Court and strip it of jurisdiction over public-education cases failed, and [Chief Justice] Earl Warren finished his service without impeachment. During the Watergate scandal, a United States Supreme Court with four [Richard] Nixon appointees required the president to honor a subpoena directing him to produce tape recordings of his conversations with advisors in the White House. President Nixon provided the documents, and then promptly resigned. Sued while in office by Paula Jones, President [Bill] Clinton asked the Court to stay the court proceedings until the expiration of his term, asserting immunity. The Supreme Court dismissed his petition, and finally, in the cliffhanger presidential election of 2000, the Supreme Court decided which votes to count. Despite the immense controversy, [Al] Gore congratulated [George W.] Bush, and the nation went on with its business.

That is probably the best-case scenario, the best judicial system in the world at some of its finest hours. To know the value of an independent judiciary, we really should look at the worst case scenario as well, where the judiciary is completely dependent. If you're interested, read the book *Hitler's Justice* by Ingo Muller.

Not approaching that travesty, we do have recurring problems in three or four areas which, somewhat like the picture on a puzzle box, suggest a pattern in the challenges to judicial independence. The facets and hues of each of the areas blend together however, like the colors and textures they use in jigsaw puzzles. You have to study the pieces to see how they fit. The concepts involved are: public hostility and unjustified criticism by media; the judicial selection process; political challenge through manipulation of judicial system; and public confidence issues.

Criticism of the Judiciary

First on the list, criticism of the judiciary soars like the American eagle today. Type in judicial activism on the your Internet search engine. Be prepared! One of the most ardent [critics], Phyllis Schlafly, a self-appointed expert on the Constitution and judiciary, describes the federal bench as the biggest threat to constitutional government today, and charges "The entire existence of our constitutional republic hangs in the balance. We have suffered half a century of activist/liberal court decisions that seriously threaten to undermine our Rule of Law." Phyllis Schlafly is polite compared to most.

Criticism is an American pastime. We pay television performers to tear apart the real life performances of others. We cannot expect in this era of satellites and cell phones to be free from criticism. Even before all that, as early 1787, Thomas Jefferson wrote, ". . . were it left to me to decide whether we should have a government without newspapers, or newspapers without a government, I should not hesitate a moment to prefer the latter."

What then is the problem with all this noise about judges? Florida Judge George Greer gives a wonderful example. He is a Republican, so conservative that some websites question his impartiality for the bench. Yet in his response to the case of Terri Schiavo [a Florida woman who had been in a persistent vegetative state for a number of years and whose husband in 1998 petitioned the Florida courts to have his wife's feeding tube removed], Greer, a regular churchgoer, gained the wrath of the religious right. His decision allowing removal of the feeding tube placed him in the middle of a controversy over the sanctity of life.

Rules of judicial conduct required his answer: Silence. "The really difficult part of this job," Greer said, "is that you can't defend yourself." Often misinformation drives the public stories and letters to the editor. Judges attacked by false or misleading criticisms need help to correct factually inaccurate records, and to avoid an appearance that the judge caused the injustice. They need support to continue functioning in their independent responsibilities. Judge Greer, for example, issued a steady series of rulings despite being targeted for electoral defeat and impeachment, being compared to Joseph Mengele and other Nazis, and even being threatened with death.

The American Bar Association has developed model programs for bar associations and court administrators to support the judiciary in this regard. Wisconsin has such a program through the Director's Office, and it has acted in several cases where judges called for assistance. . . .

Criticism Has Consequences

Often, the hostility and animosity evident through media responses, and letters to the editor roll over and become political campaigns. Judicial selection processes dominate independence concerns. Controversial elections in California challenged Chief Justice Rose Bird and two other justices on the [state] Supreme Court. They all lost retention elections which revolved around death penalty cases. In 1996, Tennessee Supreme Court justice Penny White also lost a retention election over a death penalty case. It doesn't require the death penalty to create hostile judicial campaigns. These are only a few of many instances.

Judicial Independence

Simply stated, judicial independence is the ability of a judge to decide a matter free from pressures or inducements. Additionally, the institution of the judiciary as a whole must also be independent by being separate from government and other concentrations of power. The principal role of an independent judiciary is to uphold the rule of law and to ensure the supremacy of the law. If the judiciary is to exercise a truly impartial and independent adjudicative function, it must have special powers to allow it to "keep its distance" from other governmental institutions, political organisations, and other non-governmental influences, and to be free of repercussions from such outside influences.

F.B. William Kelly,
"An Independent Judiciary:
The Core of the Rule of Law,"
International Centre for Criminal Justice
Reform and Criminal Justice Policy, *2002.*

Money plays a huge role in the outcome of these cases. In a recent race for a seat on the Supreme Court in tiny West Virginia, the candidates and their supporters spent $5 million. Trial lawyers and unions supported the incumbent [Warren] McGraw. His opponent, [Brent] Benjamin, courted big business and big coal. Donald Blankenship, the CEO [chief executive officer] of the largest coal producer in the region, became a major backer. The company faced a major lawsuit headed to the Supreme Court. Blankenship set a modern record for an individual contribution to a judicial race with approximately $3.5 million spent, about $2 for every person in the state. His candidate won with attack ads and automated phone calls.

The Brennan Center for Justice follows trends and expenses in judicial campaigns. Spending from special interest groups in judicial campaigns has tripled since the 2002 elections. Proposed tort reforms and medical malpractice insurance drive the debates, and secure the money. The U.S. Chamber of Commerce has spent millions along with other special interest groups. The new record for two candidates? Approximately ten million dollars expended in an Illinois Supreme Court race.

Reforms of the System

Some states have accomplished successful reforms. Financial disclosure laws emphasize special-interest spending; voter guides provide the public with independent campaign information; North Carolina publically finances judicial elections, and thus eliminates 3rd party advertisements. A similar Wisconsin effort lags behind although recently efforts have been renewed. North Carolina also requires black out periods on ads before the elections, and prohibits telephone banks and mass mailings.

Political Manipulation

The disputes extend beyond elections to the appointment process as well. We can't watch the news lately [2005] without hearing of the "nuclear option" and I'm not talking about North Korea, but the rules on filibusters in the Senate. The Senate majority leader, Bill Frist, . . . appeared on a telecast of a religious organization with the message that those opposing judicial nominations are conducting an assault "against people of faith." The dispute rage[d] over about 7 of President [George W.] Bush's 205 nominees. Senate Minority Leader Harry Reid has promised to grind the work of the Senate to a halt if the filibuster rules are changed.

If politicians can't change the people in power, they work on the process. It's important to recall that political manipulation of the judiciary isn't a new game. Until 1867, the jurisdiction of federal courts expanded. Then, on a November night, military officers arrested a man named McCardle, the editor of the *Vicksburg [Mississippi] Times*. His criticism of the military occupation of Southern states led to charges for disturbing the peace and inciting insurrection. His habeas corpus petition [to determine if he was lawfully detained] ended up in the United States Supreme Court. Congress acted quickly to repeal the law that allowed the Supreme Court to hear the case, and the Court then dismissed the appeal. It was the first time Congress had acted to limit the authority of the courts.

Under the Constitution, Congress establishes the lower federal courts, and can make "exceptions" and "regulations" for the Supreme Court's jurisdiction as well. The McCardle decision, coupled with the exceptions clause, allows congressmen to claim they can make a Supreme Court of one person and a card table, and do away with all the other federal courts. It's not quite that simple. Many scholars and jurists argue that Congress may only enact laws about the process or procedure of jurisdiction rather than controlling substantive outcomes.

Despite that, the battle rages on. During the Schiavo case, House Majority Leader Tom DeLay warned that, "no little judge sitting in a state district court in Florida is going to usurp the authority of Congress." He sponsored legislation which allowed federal review of the state court decision without regard to issue or claim preclusion. After her death, he issued an inferred threat to any judge who may have come near the case. "Mrs. Schiavo's death is a moral poverty and a legal tragedy. This loss happened because our legal system did not protect the people who need protection most, and that will change. The time will come for the men responsible for this to answer for their behavior, but not today."

Shortly after the incident, The Judeo-Christian Council for Constitutional Reform held widely publicized judicial reform conference in Washington, DC. They held a news conference to announce a Declaration in Support of Tom DeLay. The Declaration read:

> The conservative movement . . . is uniting behind House Majority Tom DeLay. Specifically, the Declaration endorses DeLay's call for judicial reform. Echoing the words of Franklin Delano Roosevelt, signers of the Declaration are saying, "We must save the Constitution from the Court and the Court from itself."

The Supreme Court and the New Deal

Although it's hard to appreciate how anything might engender the intensity or animosity that [the Schiavo case did], their Declaration refers to a situation that came close. By 1936 Roosevelt's legislation had created such a panoply of government agencies for public support that their acronyms came to be known as alphabet soup. Although wildly popular with a public suffering from the Depression, the Supreme Court majority at the time believed the actions to be unconstitutional invasions of the right to contract. When the Court declared the Agricultural Adjustment Act unconstitutional, public protests erupted. The six members on the majority opinion [were] hung in effigy in Ames, IA.

Fearing the Supreme Court would strike down the Social Security program and the National Labor Relations Act, Roosevelt attempted to "pack the court." He asked Congress to appoint an additional justice to the Supreme Court for any member of the court over age 70 who didn't retire. He claimed the issue of the productivity of aged or infirm judges affected the burdens of the federal courts. It touched off a constitutional controversy not seen since the creation of the Republic. At the Senate Judiciary Committee, a Harvard law professor testified, "There are at least two ways of getting rid of judges. One is to take them out and shoot them, as they are reported to do in at least one other country. The other way is more genteel, but no less effective. They are kept on the public payroll but their votes are cancelled." Many suggested that Roosevelt was adopting the tactics of fascism. Both sides believed the future of the country was at stake.

Two unexpected events averted the controversy. One justice switched positions on the issues, and another conservative justice unexpectedly retired, giving Roosevelt a majority on the court. With no further risk to his legislative program, the attempt to pack the court died. Roosevelt lost the battle, but won a struggle to legitimize a greatly expanded exercise of power by government.

The Importance of an Impartial Judiciary

This exercise of powers drives the ire of those who push for limits on the court today, but the principle involved remains the same. That principle established more than two hundred years ago requires an independent judiciary to maintain liberty through the rule of law. The principle is more important than political power or process. It requires what Judge Learned Hand [a twentieth-century U.S. district and appellate judge] called a spirit of moderation:

> What is the spirit of moderation? It is the temper which does not press a partisan advantage to its bitter end, which can understand and will respect the other side, which feels a unity between all citizens—real and not the factitious product of propaganda—which recognizes their common fate and common aspirations—in a word, which has faith in the sacredness of the individual.

[Wisconsin] Chief Justice [Shirley] Abrahamson had a recent article in the *Wisconsin Lawyer*. She stated: "The basic underlying safeguard for judicial independence is popular support for the concept."

Periodical Bibliography

The following articles have been selected to supplement the diverse views presented in this chapter.

David F. Forte — "Appealing to the Judge's Better Angels," Heritage Lecture #1111, Heritage Foundation, February 19, 2009. www.heritage.org/research/legalissues/hl1111.cfm.

Jonathan Hafetz — "Supreme Court Deals Death Blow to Gitmo," *Nation*, June 12, 2008. www.thenation.com/doc/20080630/hafetz.

Hugh Hewitt — "The United States Supreme Court Versus America: Awarding the Privilege of Habeas Corpus to Terrorists," *Townhall.com*, June 12, 2008. http://townhall.com/columnists/HughHewitt/2008/06/12/the_united_states_supreme_court_versus_america_awarding_the_privilege_of_habeas_corpus_to_terrorists.

Aziz Huq — "Justice Delayed and Denied at Guantanamo," *Nation*, September 29, 2008. www.thenation.com/doc/20081013/huq.

Scott Lemieux — "Beyond Boumediene," *American Prospect*, June 16, 2008. www.prospect.org/cs/articles?article=beyond_boumediene.

Robert A. Levy — "Habeas Half-Truths: Do the Critics of *Boumediene v. Bush* Have a Case?" *Reason*, July 2, 2008. www.reason.com/news/show/127285.html.

Andy Worthington — "The Supreme Court's Gitmo Decision," *CounterPunch*, June 13–15, 2008. www.counterpunch.org/worthington06132008.html.

OPPOSING
VIEWPOINTS®
SERIES

CHAPTER 2

How Should the U.S. Supreme Court Rule on Moral and Religious Issues?

Chapter Preface

In 1970, attorneys Linda Coffee and Sarah Weddington filed a lawsuit on behalf of Norma L. McCorvey in U.S. District Court. The lawsuit argued that Texas laws outlawing abortion unless a mother's life was in danger violated their client's rights. McCorvey, more widely known by her pseudonym "Jane Roe," claimed that she had gotten pregnant as a result of a rape and wanted to safely and legally terminate her pregnancy. The court ruled in McCorvey's favor but refused to grant an injunction against the enforcement of the Texas law. The ruling was appealed to the U.S. Supreme Court. On January 22, 1973, the Court announced its decision on the appeal: they sided with Roe and struck down the Texas law as unconstitutional, which resulted in making abortion services safer and more accessible to women. It also established *Roe v. Wade* as one of the most controversial and widely discussed legal decisions in U.S. judicial history.

The Court's decision in *Roe v. Wade* was based on years of case law that established that the government cannot interfere with certain personal decisions about marriage, procreation, and other facets of life. One of those cases was *Griswold v. Connecticut* (1965), in which the Court struck down a Connecticut statute that prohibited doctors and family-planning clinics from providing contraceptives to married couples. In that decision, the Court established a right to privacy, which allowed the couple to make their own family planning decisions. Seven years later, the Court decided in *Eisenstadt v. Baird* that single people have the same right to privacy.

Opponents of *Roe v. Wade* objected that the Court's decision lacked a valid constitutional foundation, noting that the U.S. Constitution does not directly address the issue. Therefore, opponents assert, the most appropriate way to deal with the problem would be through laws passed by state legislatures and through the democratic process—not a sweeping ruling from the Supreme Court. Abortion opponents lobbied state and federal lawmakers to pass anti-abortion laws or to severely restrict access to abortions. Many of these restrictions limited or eliminated state and federal funding for abortions or established requirements that girls under 18 years of age obtain the consent of their parents prior to an abortion. Since the *Roe* decision, a number of these laws have been brought before the Court; some have been struck down because the Court decided they violated a woman's right to privacy, while others have been upheld by the Court.

Because of the central role the Supreme Court plays in the abortion issue, nominees to the Court are asked their opinions on *Roe v. Wade* for any clue as to how they might rule if new abortion cases come before the Court. Prior cases decided by potential justices are parsed, discussed, interpreted, and debated to discover what a potential justice will do. As both sides—choice supporters and abortion opponents—jockey to either protect or eliminate the right to abortion services in the United States, the controversy about the Court's role in the matter continues to rage.

The viewpoints collected in the following chapter explore the debate over how the Supreme Court should approach issues of morality and religion. Specifically discussed are the Court's decisions regarding *Roe v. Wade* as well as in limiting the role of religion in government domains.

> *"For the Supreme Court to say that government can no longer legislate to protect morality and family life would be suicidal."*

The U.S. Supreme Court Should Uphold Sodomy Laws

Robert Peters

Robert Peters is the president of Morality in Media, a conservative group that informs citizens and the media about pornography and advocates for stronger antipornography laws. In the following viewpoint, Peters argues that by striking down the Texas sodomy law in Lawrence v. Texas *[2003], the Supreme Court extended the right to privacy to a sexual act, sodomy, which had been considered a crime for decades in the United States and was found to be a crime by the Supreme Court in a 1986 case,* Hardwick v. Bowers. *He also maintains that the Court and the government have the right to rule on and legislate morality.*

As you read, consider the following questions:

1. Why does the author believe the government has a legitimate interest in protecting morality?

Robert Peters, "Morality: Is It the Business of Government?" *Concerned Women for America*, July 16, 2003. Reproduced by permission.

2. What does the author cite as the "incalculable amount of harm" done to society because of heterosexual promiscuity and homosexual sodomy?

3. What did Justice Antonin Scalia say in his dissent of *Lawrence v. Texas*?

It is often said (at least by some) that in the United States, "You can't legislate morality."

As defined in *Webster's New World Dictionary*, morality is defined as "rightness or wrongness, as of an action." For example, in the U.S. it is considered wrong to:

- murder someone;

- steal someone's wallet, laptop computer or car;

- perjure yourself;

- commit treason;

- traffic in heroin or crack cocaine;

- own slaves;

- deny someone a job because of his or her race, ethnic origin, religion or gender;

- harass or threaten someone;

- incite a riot;

- market products with dangerous defects;

- pollute streams, rivers and lakes;

- engage in "insider trading."

The list could go on and on. Despite what some may say, therefore, as a general principle we can and do make moral judgments about certain behaviors—and we do legislate against them.

What Naysayers Really Mean

Perhaps then, what the naysayers mean is that we can't legislate *sexual* morality.

But if that were true, then we could no longer enact or enforce laws (including laws pertaining to adoption, child custody and divorce) pertaining to sexual behaviors such as adultery, bestiality, bigamy, child pornography, fornication, "gay marriage," incest, obscenity, polygamy, the distribution of pornography to children, prostitution, public lewdness (as in two adults copulating in the middle of a public park at 12 noon), rape, sexual molestation of children, sexual harassment on the job, and the opening of a strip joint adjacent to an elementary or high school.

Perhaps then, what is really meant is that we can't legislate sexual morality *in the bedroom.*

But if that were true, we could no longer apply any laws (including laws pertaining to adoption, child custody and divorce) pertaining to sexual behaviors—such as adultery, bestiality, bigamy, fornication, "gay marriage," incest, polygamy, prostitution, date or statutory rape, sexual molestation of children, or sexual behaviors that endanger the lives of participants—when the conduct takes place in the bedroom.

Perhaps then, what is really, really meant is that we can't legislate sexual morality in the bedroom *when it involves consenting adults only.*

But if that were true, we could no longer apply any laws (including laws pertaining to adoption, child custody and divorce) pertaining to sexual behaviors (such as adultery, bigamy, possession of child pornography, fornication, "gay marriage," incest, polygamy, prostitution, or sexual behaviors that endanger the lives of participants) when the behavior takes place in the bedroom and involves consenting adults only.

Lawrence v. Texas

In June 2003, the United States Supreme Court in *Lawrence v. Texas* held that the Texas sodomy law was unconstitutional as applied to "adult sexual intimacy in the home." In so holding, the Court extended the "right of privacy"—which cannot be found in the text of the Constitution—to a sexual behavior, sodomy, which has been a crime for centuries and that in 1986 was found by the Supreme Court in *Hardwick v. Bowers* to be unprotected by the Constitution.

Writing for the majority, Justice [Anthony] Kennedy said that *Lawrence* was about whether "petitioners were free as adults to engage in private conduct in the exercise of their liberty under the Due Process Clause of the Fourteenth Amendment." Later, Justice Kennedy said the Texas law touched upon "the most private human conduct, sexual behavior, and in the most private of places, the home." Later still, Justice Kennedy said the case involves "two adults who, with full and mutual consent from each other, engaged in sexual practices common to a homosexual lifestyle."

At one point Justice Kennedy opined:

> [F]or centuries there have been powerful voices to condemn homosexual conduct as immoral. The condemnation has been shaped by religious beliefs, conceptions of right and acceptable behavior, and respect for the traditional family.... The issue is whether the majority may use the power of the State to enforce these views on the whole society through operation of the criminal law. "Our obligation is to define the liberty of all, not to mandate our own moral code."

Justice Kennedy quoted Justice [John Paul] Stevens in an earlier case for the proposition that "the fact that the governing majority in a State has traditionally viewed a particular practice as immoral is not a sufficient reason for upholding a law prohibiting a practice." Justice Kennedy then concluded that the Texas statute "furthers no legitimate state interest which can justify its intrusion into the personal and private life of the individual."

In a justifiably angry dissent, Justice [Antonin] Scalia wrote:

> The Texas statute undeniably seeks to further the belief of its citizens that certain forms of sexual behavior are "immoral and unacceptable"—[*Hardwick v. Bowers*]—the same interest furthered by criminal laws against fornication, bigamy, adultery, adult incest, bestiality, and obscenity. *Bowers* held that this was a legitimate state interest. The Court today reaches the opposite conclusion. . . . This effectively decrees the end of all morals legislation. If . . . the promotion of majoritarian sexual morality is not even a *legitimate* state interest, none of the above-mentioned laws can survive rational basis review.

A Narrower Reading of the Case

In *Paris Adult Theatre I v. Slaton*, the Supreme Court recognized that there are "legitimate governmental interests at stake in stemming the tide of commercialized obscenity, even assuming it is feasible to enforce effective safeguards against exposure to juveniles. . . ." (It goes without saying that we have failed miserably in erecting and enforcing 'safeguards against exposure to juveniles,' but that is the subject of another article.)

The "legitimate governmental interests" alluded to by the *Paris* Court include the right of the government to "maintain a decent society" and to protect:

- "the quality of life and total community environment";

- "public safety";

- "the social interest in order *and morality*"; and

- "*family life*". [Emphasis added.]

Lawrence will undoubtedly be cited for the proposition that government no longer has a legitimate interest in protecting "morality" or "family life." Morality and family life, however, are essential for the well-being of any society. For the Supreme Court to say that government can no longer legislate to protect morality and family life would be suicidal.

What the Supreme Court has said is that if government passes criminal legislation to control what goes on in the bedroom of consenting adults, it must have a justification other than the majority's belief that a particular sexual behavior is morally wrong.

The *Paris* Court Opinion

As noted above, the *Paris* Court indicated that the state could act to protect the "social interest in order and morality." Later in its opinion, the *Paris* Court also had this to say:

> The issue in this context goes beyond whether someone, or even the majority, considers the [hardcore sexual] conduct "wrong" or "sinful." The States have the power to make a morally neutral judgment that public exhibition of obscene material, or commerce in such material, has a tendency to injure the community as a whole, to endanger the public safety, or to jeopardize, in Mr. Chief Justice [Earl] Warren's words, the State's "right to maintain a decent society."

Some will argue that the Paris Court first approved and then disapproved of the notion that states can act to protect "morality." I would argue that the Court is simply making a distinction based on the justification for protecting morality. In the first instance, government is prohibiting the distribution of obscenity because obscenity undermines morality, which leads to promiscuity, abortions, single-parent families, adultery and more single-parent families, sexually transmitted diseases, sexual abuse of children, and rape. In the second instance, government is prohibiting the distribution of obscenity simply because a majority believe it is "wrong" or "sinful."

It should also be noted that in *Stanley v. Georgia* (1969), the Supreme Court held that the "mere private possession of obscenity cannot constitutionally be made a crime"; and in so holding, said in part: "Whatever may be the justifications for other statutes regulating obscenity, we do not think they reach into the privacy of the home."

What About Public Indecency Laws?

In his dissent, Justice Scalia noted that in *Barnes v. Glen Theatre* (1991), the Supreme Court concluded that Indiana's public indecency statute furthered a "substantial government interest in protecting order and morality" and was therefore called into question by the Court's decision in *Lawrence v. Texas*.

What occurs in a public place (e.g., people walking down the middle of a busy street with no clothes on), however, often raises concerns that are not raised when the same behavior takes place in private. While *Boston Beer Co. v. Massachusetts* (1878), was not directly in point, it did state a principle worth noting:

> Whatever differences of opinion might exist as to the extent and boundaries of the police power . . . there seems to be no doubt that it does extend to the preservation of good order and *public* morals. [Emphasis added.]

In his concurring opinion in *Barnes v. Glen Theatre*, Justice [David] Souter also said that the Indiana public indecency law could constitutionally be applied to strip joints because of the "State's substantial interest in combating the secondary effects of adult entertainment establishments of the sort typified by respondents' establishments."

Interestingly, Justice Souter raised this argument even though "this justification has not been articulated by Indiana's legislature or its courts." One is left to wonder then, why the Supreme Court in *Lawrence v. Texas* didn't look to justifica-

How Justices' Social Views Impact Their Decisions

All too often, judicial reasoning comes down to the justice's or judge's whims, prejudices, ideology or personal philosophy of life and the universe. The Constitution becomes mere window dressing for forcing their values on a cringing public.

The classic example of this is Justice Sandra Day O'Connor's shifting position in the two Supreme Court cases dealing with state anti-sodomy laws. In 1986, in *Bowers v. Hardwick*, O'Connor sided with the majority in holding that there was nothing in the Constitution prohibiting a state from making homosexual sex a crime. In 2003, in *Lawrence v. Texas*, she again sided with the majority—this time, determining that the Constitution most certainly did preclude anti-sodomy statutes. What was it about the Constitution that O'Connor did not understand in 1986 that she suddenly comprehended in 2003? It wasn't the Constitution that changed in those 17 years, or even O'Connor's understanding of the Constitution. What changed were O'Connor's social views, which she then read into the Constitution.

That's how Constitutional law is unmade by activist judges.

Den Feder,
"Do Conservatives 'Openly Threaten Sitting Judges'?"
FrontPage.Magazine.com, April 19, 2005.

tions for the Texas sodomy statute other than majority sentiments about homosexual sodomy. For example, one *amicus* [friend of the court] brief forcefully argued that the Texas law was justifiable as a public health measure.

Other 'Consenting' Behaviors

With regard to adultery and bigamy, we are not talking just about consenting adults. Rarely does an innocent spouse consent to a marriage partner's infidelity, and children are also typically involved. Women's groups can also be expected to set forth valid reasons why polygamy is properly prohibited in the United States. Marriage is also a public institution.

With regard to bestiality, we are not talking at all about consenting adults. Animal rights groups will also argue forcefully that bestiality is rightly a crime, whether the conduct takes place in the woods, the field, the barn, the zoo, or the bedroom.

With regard to fornication, it is difficult to imagine the High Court holding that adult homosexuals have a right to have sex in private, but not heterosexual adults. The Court's privacy right concerns notwithstanding, however, it is nevertheless clear that since the outbreak of the so-called sexual revolution, heterosexual promiscuity and homosexual sodomy have caused an incalculable amount of harm to society in terms of abortions, divorce, single-parent families, sexually transmitted diseases (including AIDS), sexual abuse of children and rape.

Even assuming the Constitution should protect the right of adults to engage in sodomy in private, it does not follow that the State should also be required to formally recognize that private conduct as a "marriage." While the cases are not directly in point, it should also be noted that the Supreme Court rejected the argument that the right to possess obscenity in the home gives rise to a correlative right to obtain it in the marketplace. See, *United States v. Thirty-Seven Photographs*, (1971) and *State v. Burgin*, (1971). Consider also what may be next if the High Court holds in a future case that adults in the privacy of the home have a right to bugger farm animals.

Incest may prove to be a difficult case, especially where same-sex couples are involved. Historically, incest has been prohibited in large measure because of concerns about genetics.

Prostitution, like distribution of obscenity, is a commercial enterprise with a public dimension. Furthermore, law enforcement agencies rarely if ever attempt to get a search warrant to enter the home or hotel room of the customer.

Concluding Thoughts

What prompted me to write this article was not my disagreement with the holding in *Lawrence* but rather my concern that morally blind proponents of the hellish sexual revolution, both on the Court and off, will try to make more of this case than they should.

Narrowly read, *Lawrence v. Texas* stands for the proposition that majority views about right and wrong—especially, if religious based—standing alone, are not a sufficient basis to prohibit consenting adult homosexuals from engaging privately in sexual conduct.

Presumably, private means private. Private does not mean conduct that takes place in public places. Private also does not mean public recognition—as in requiring states to bestow upon homosexual relationships the same status as heterosexual marriages. In his majority opinion, Justice Kennedy was careful to point out that *Lawrence*:

> ... does not involve minors. It does not involve persons who might be injured or coerced or are situated in relationships where consent might not easily be refused. It does not involve public conduct or prostitution. It does not involve whether the government must give formal recognition to any relationship that homosexual persons seek to enter.

I would add that our nation's Founding Fathers also believed in the right of privacy. That is why we have the Fourth

Amendment that protects the "right of the people to be secure in their persons, houses, papers, and effects, against unreasonable searches and seizures."

As is often the case, however, when the plain limits of the Constitution do not fit with the private notions of Supreme Court justices, they simply bypass the American people and in effect "amend" the Constitution by creating rights that do not exist in the text of the Constitution or by interpreting provisions to mean what they were never intended to mean. Either Supreme justices (like other federal officials) are *under* the Constitution—or they *are* the Constitution.

Now, it should be said that many people who believe that homosexual behavior is morally wrong and that the "gay rights" movement is in general a destructive movement also believed that laws prohibiting acts of sodomy between consenting adults in private places were unwise and should have been repealed by the various legislatures.

That is the subject for another article. But I will add my voice to those who say that in *Lawrence v. Texas* the Supreme Court once again entered the legislative realm of policy making. As Justice Scalia put it in his dissent, the Supreme Court has:

> ... largely signed on to the so-called homosexual agenda, by which I mean the agenda promoted by homosexual activists directed at eliminating the moral opprobrium that has traditionally attached to homosexual conduct. . . . It is clear . . . that the Court has taken sides in the cultural war departing from its role as a neutral observer.

> *"A doctrine allowing legislation to be justified solely on the basis of morality would recognize an unlimited police power in state legislatures. Unlimited power is the very definition of tyranny."*

The U.S. Supreme Court Should Reverse Sodomy Laws

Randy E. Barnett

Randy E. Barnett is a Washington, D.C., based legal scholar, law professor at Georgetown University Law Center, and senior fellow at the Cato Institute, a libertarian think tank. In the following viewpoint, Barnett maintains that Lawrence v. Texas *was correctly decided because the Supreme Court held that same-sex sexual freedom is a legitimate aspect of liberty rather than being protected as a right to privacy. Barnett argues that government prohibition of conduct on grounds of immorality leads to tyranny. He contends the ruling was revolutionary in that it employs a "presumption of liberty" and calls upon the government to justify any statute that restricts liberty.*

Randy E. Barnett, "Justice Kennedy's Libertarian Revolution: *Lawrence v. Texas*," *Cato Supreme Court Review*, vol. 123, 2002–2003. Copyright © 2002–2003. Republished with permission of CATO Institute, conveyed through Copyright Clearance Center, Inc.

As you read, consider the following questions:

1. According to the author, the *Lawrence* decision did not protect "a right of privacy," but instead protected what?

2. What was the role of liberty in Justice Anthony Kennedy's majority opinion on *Lawrence v. Texas*, as described by the author?

3. Why does the author believe the *Lawrence* decision is potentially revolutionary?

In *Lawrence v. Texas*, the Supreme Court held unconstitutional a Texas law criminalizing sexual relations between persons of the same sex. That would be reason enough to consider the case a landmark decision. But to those schooled in post-New Deal "fundamental rights" jurisprudence, what was most striking about *Lawrence* was the *way* the Court justified its ruling. If the approach the Court took in the case is followed in other cases in the future, we have in *Lawrence* nothing short of a constitutional revolution, with implications reaching far beyond the "personal liberty" at issue here.

Contrary to how their decision was widely reported, the *Lawrence* majority did not protect a "right of privacy." Instead, quite simply, they protected "liberty." Breaking free at last of the post-New Deal constitutional tension between the "presumption of constitutionality," on one hand, and "fundamental rights," on the other, Justice Anthony Kennedy and the four justices who joined his opinion did not begin by assuming the statute was constitutional. But neither did they call the liberty at issue "fundamental," which the modern Court would have been expected to do before withholding the presumption of constitutionality from the statute. Instead, the Court took the much simpler tack of requiring the state to justify its statute, whatever the status of the right at issue. . . .

Justice Kennedy's Crucial Switch from Privacy to Liberty

In the 1992 abortion rights case of *Planned Parenthood v. Casey*, Justice Kennedy began to escape from the New Deal-era box in the part of the coauthored opinion that is commonly attributed to him. He refused there to rest abortion rights on a "right to privacy," although that crucial move has been generally ignored. Instead, he rested those rights on liberty and explicitly on the Ninth Amendment:

> Neither the Bill of Rights nor the specific practices of States at the time of the adoption of the Fourteenth Amendment marks the outer limits of the substantive sphere of *liberty* which the Fourteenth Amendment protects. See U.S. Const., Amend. 9.

Resting abortion rights on liberty, as opposed to privacy, was newsworthy, but little noticed. To this day, most scholars and public commentators still speak of the "right of privacy," not the "right of liberty." Until *Lawrence*, the question was whether this right to liberty would ever be seen again.

In *Lawrence v. Texas*, it has reappeared, with Justice Kennedy now writing for a majority of the Court (not including Justice [Sandra Day] O'Connor, who concurred only in the result), rather than as part of a mere trio in *Casey*. Liberty, not privacy, pervades this opinion like none other, beginning with the very first paragraph:

> *Liberty* protects the person from unwarranted government intrusions into a dwelling or other private places. In our tradition the State is not omnipresent in the home. And there are other spheres of our lives and existence, outside the home, where the State should not be a dominant presence. Freedom extends beyond spatial bounds. *Liberty* presumes an autonomy of self that includes freedom of thought, belief, expression, and certain intimate conduct. The instant case involves *liberty* of the person both in its spatial and more transcendent dimensions.

Other examples abound:

> We conclude the case should be resolved by determining whether the petitioners were free as adults to engage in the private conduct in the exercise of their *liberty* under the Due Process Clause of the Fourteenth Amendment to the Constitution.

> There are broad statements of the substantive reach of *liberty* under the Due Process Clause in earlier [Progressive-era] cases, including *Pierce v. Society of Sisters* (1925), and *Meyer v. Nebraska* (1923); but the most pertinent beginning point is our decision in *Griswold v. Connecticut* (1965).

Justice Kennedy puts rhetorical distance between the decision in *Lawrence* and the right of privacy protected in *Griswold*: "The Court [in *Griswold*] described the protected interest as a right to privacy and placed emphasis on the marriage relation and the protected space of the marital bedroom." Indeed, the "right of privacy" makes no other appearance in this opinion (apart from quotations from the grant of certiorari [a writ of superior court to call up the records of an inferior court] from a previous case discussing *Griswold*). In contrast "liberty" appears in the opinion at least twenty-five times.

Even Justice Kennedy's rejection of the argument from *stare decisis* [the policy of standing by prior rulings] rests on the centrality of liberty.

> In *Casey* we noted that when a Court is asked to overrule a precedent recognizing a constitutional liberty interest, individual or societal reliance on the existence of that liberty cautions with particular strength against reversing course. . . . The holding in *Bowers* [*v. Hardwick*], however, has not induced detrimental reliance comparable to some instances where recognized individual rights are involved.

In *Lawrence v. Texas*, therefore, liberty, not privacy, is doing all the work.

Justice Kennedy Employs an Implicit "Presumption of Liberty"

Lawrence is potentially revolutionary not only because it abandons a right to privacy in favor of liberty, but for another closely related reason: In the majority's opinion, there is not even the pretense of a "fundamental right" rebutting the "presumption of constitutionality." Justice Kennedy never mentions any presumption to be accorded the Texas statute.

More important, he never tries to justify the sexual liberty of same-sex couples as a fundamental right. Instead, he spends all of his energies demonstrating that same-sex sexual freedom is a legitimate aspect of liberty—unlike, for example, actions that violate the rights of others, which are not liberty but license. [This removes the Court] from the framework of unenumerated fundamental rights that was engrafted upon it in the wake of *Griswold*. Until *Lawrence*, every unenumerated rights case had to establish that the liberty at issue was "fundamental," as opposed to a mere liberty interest.

Justice [Antonin] Scalia, in dissent, takes accurate note of all of this:

> Though there is discussion of "fundamental proposition[s]," . . . and "fundamental decisions," . . . nowhere does the Court's opinion declare that homosexual sodomy is a "fundamental right" under the Due Process Clause; nor does it subject the Texas law to the standard of review that would be appropriate (strict scrutiny) if homosexual sodomy were a "fundamental right." Thus, while overruling the outcome of *Bowers*, the Court leaves strangely untouched its central legal conclusion: "[R]espondent would have us announce . . . a fundamental right to engage in homosexual sodomy. This we are quite unwilling to do." Instead the Court simply describes petitioners' conduct as "an exercise of their liberty"—which it undoubtedly is—and proceeds to apply an unheard-of form of rational-basis review that will have far-reaching implications beyond this case.

In other words, with liberty as the baseline, the majority places the onus on the government to justify its statutory restriction.

Although he never acknowledges it, Justice Kennedy is employing here what I have called a "presumption of liberty" that requires the government to justify its restriction on liberty, instead of requiring the citizen to establish that the liberty being exercised is somehow "fundamental." In this way, once an action is deemed to be a proper exercise of liberty (as opposed to license), the burden shifts to the government.

All that was offered by the government to justify this statute is the judgment of the legislature that the prohibited conduct is "immoral," which for the majority (including, on this issue, Justice O'Connor) is simply not enough to justify the restriction of liberty. Why not? Here the Court is content to rest its conclusion on a quote from Justice [John Paul] Stevens's dissenting opinion in *Bowers*:

> Our prior cases make two propositions abundantly clear. First, the fact that the governing majority in a State has traditionally viewed a particular practice as immoral is not a sufficient reason for upholding a law prohibiting the practice; neither history nor tradition could save a law prohibiting miscegenation [a mixture of races, usually in reference to marriage between a white person and a member of another race] from constitutional attack. Second, individual decisions by married persons, concerning the intimacies of their physical relationship, even when not intended to produce offspring, are a form of "liberty" protected by the Due Process Clause of the Fourteenth Amendment. Moreover, this protection extends to intimate choices by unmarried as well as married persons.

A stronger defense of this conclusion is possible. A legislative judgment of "immorality" means simply that a majority of the legislature disapproves of this conduct. But justifying legislation solely on grounds of morality would entirely eliminate judicial review of legislative powers. How could a court ever adjudicate between a legislature's claim that a particular exercise of liberty is "immoral" and a defendant's contrary claim that it is not?

In practice, therefore, a doctrine allowing legislation to be justified solely on the basis of morality would recognize an unlimited police power in state legislatures. Unlimited power is the very definition of tyranny. Although the police power of states may be broad, it was never thought to be unlimited.

Defending *Lawrence* from Judicial Conservatives

Given their grounding still rooted in post-New Deal constitutional jurisprudence, the responses of judicial conservatives (not to be equated with all *political* conservatives) are entirely predictable. Yet each fails upon critical inspection. Three such responses stand out.

First, judicial conservatives argue that all laws restrict some freedom; thus, requiring legislatures to justify to a court their restrictions on liberty would amount to giving judges an unbridled power to strike down laws of which they disapprove. But that is to equate "liberty" and "license," a mistake the Founders never made. Liberty is and always has been the *properly defined* exercise of freedom. Liberty is and always has been constrained by the rights of others. No one's genuine right to liberty is violated by restricting his or her freedom to rape or murder, because there is no such right in the first place.

That is not to say that the rightful exercise of liberty may never be *regulated*—or made regular (as opposed to prohibited outright). It is only to say that, as Justice Kennedy implicitly acknowledges, the existence of a right to liberty places a burden on the government to justify any regulations of liberty as necessary and proper. Wrongful behavior that violates the

The Definition of Sodomy Is Fluid

Many Americans, including some on the judiciary, assume "sodomy" is just another word for same-sex sex, and the current law in Texas—and the similar laws in Missouri, Kansas, and Oklahoma—do apply exclusively to gays and lesbians. But the majority of anti-sodomy laws, both today and in the past, apply to both heterosexual and homosexual acts. Although we now understand those acts in the main to encompass oral or anal sex, the historians point out in their brief that at different times "sodomy" has been defined to include bestiality, mutual masturbation, sex in the wrong position, sex without procreative intent, male-male, and male-female sex, though only rarely female-female. In fact, the law in force in Georgia in 1986 applied to both hetero- and homosexuals, contrary to the language of the court's opinion in *Bowers [v. Hardwick]*, which treated "sodomy" as strictly homosexual sex.

Kristin Eliasberg, "Sodomy Flaw,"
Slate.com, March 25, 2003.

rights of others may justly be prohibited without violating liberty rights—although "wrongful" is not the same as "immoral."

Second, and closely related, the *Lawrence* majority's position, judicial conservatives say, rejects any moral content of law. That is false. As was just explained, wrongful behavior that violates the rights of others may justly be prohibited without violating the liberty rights of others. Because it is usually (but not always) immoral to wrongfully violate the rights of others, the entirely justified prohibition of wrongful behavior also necessarily prohibits much immoral behavior as well. But not all ostensibly immoral behavior is also unjust or wrongful, as Thomas Aquinas [thirteenth-century Italian philosopher] recognized when he wrote:

> Now human law is framed for a number of human beings, the majority of which are not perfect in virtue. Therefore human laws do not forbid all vices, from which the virtuous abstain, but only the more grievous vices, from which it is possible for the majority to abstain, and *chiefly those that are to the hurt of others, without the prohibition of which human society could not be maintained; thus human law prohibits murder, theft and the like.*

To the claim that allowing legislatures to prohibit conduct solely because they deem it to be immoral is to grant legislatures an unlimited and therefore tyrannical power, judicial conservatives might respond that the police powers of states are to be constrained by their own constitutions and their own courts, not by federal judges. This response, if made, would be a non sequitur. On the one hand, if state constitutions grant their legislatures a "police power" that includes an unlimited power to prohibit private conduct solely because it is immoral—a dubious claim—that does not make the power any less unlimited or tyrannical. Nor in the face of such a constitutional grant of power would state judges be in any better position than federal judges to constrain their legislatures. If it is inappropriate for federal judges to restrict the asserted constitutional powers of state legislatures, it would be equally inappropriate for state judges to do so.

On the other hand, if the police power of states is not so unlimited and tyrannical as is being claimed, then it is not beyond the "judicial power" of either state or federal judges to hold state legislatures within their limits. Federal judges may do so, of course, only if they have jurisdiction to protect citizens' rights from violation by their own states. Although at the founding this power was lacking, the Privileges or Immunities Clause of the Fourteenth Amendment (which has effectively been folded into the Due Process Clause) gives the federal government such a power. Judicial conservatives must read the Fourteenth Amendment very narrowly and ahistorically to deprive federal courts of this power of judicial review.

Finally, judicial conservatives repeatedly assert that there is no textual basis for the protection of a general right to liberty. Unlike "privacy," however, "liberty" is mentioned explicitly in the Due Process Clauses of both the Fifth and Fourteenth Amendments, so this is a much harder argument to sustain. The judicial conservative response is to argue that liberty may properly be restricted so long as "due process" is followed. As Justice Scalia wrote in his dissent: "The Fourteenth Amendment *expressly allows* States to deprive their citizens of liberty, so long as due process of law is provided." This is textually and historically wrong.

Ever since the founding, "due process of law" has included judicial review to ensure that a law is within the proper power of a legislature to enact. Historical claims to the contrary are extraordinarily weak, relying exclusively (and ahistorically) on the seeming absence of an explicit grant of judicial power in the text. This fails to consider the original meaning of the "judicial power" reposed in the Supreme Court. An examination of the historical record leaves no doubt that the judicial power originally included the power to nullify unconstitutional laws—especially those that exceeded the power of the legislature.

At the federal level, judicial review, which is part of the "due process of law," includes the power to nullify laws that exceed the delegated powers of Congress. That is why the Supreme Court in *United States v. Lopez* and *United States v. Morrison* could properly strike down federal statutes that exceeded the power of Congress under the Commerce Clause. In addition, however, federal power is further constrained by the rights retained by the people—both those few that are enumerated and, as affirmed in the Ninth Amendment, those liberty rights that are unenumerated as well. At the state level, the Privileges or Immunities Clause of the Fourteenth Amendment prohibits states such as Texas from infringing the privileges or immunities of U.S. citizens. Those include both the liberty rights or "immunities" retained by the people, and the positive rights or "privileges" created by the Constitution of the United States. The "due process of law" includes federal judicial review to ensure that this constitutional restriction on the powers of states has not been transgressed.

Judicial conservatives move heaven and earth to excise the Ninth Amendment and the Privileges or Immunities Clause of the Fourteenth Amendment from the text of the Constitution because they think neither is definite enough to confine judges. That charge is only true, however, if one ignores the original public meaning of those provisions at the time of their enactment. Moreover, the Right's disregard of the text of the Constitution when it fails to support its vision of the "Rule of Law" is as much judicial "activism"—if one must use this phrase—as the Left's disregard of text when it fails to support its vision of "Justice." In either case, judges are substituting for the text something they prefer—here, silence when the Constitution is in fact speaking eloquently.

A Remarkably Simple Ruling

In the end, *Lawrence* is a very simple, indeed elegant, ruling. Justice Kennedy examined the conduct at issue to see if it was properly an aspect of liberty (as opposed to license), and then asked the government to justify its restriction, which it failed to do adequately. The decision would have been far more transparent and compelling if Kennedy had acknowledged what was really happening (though perhaps that would have lost votes by other justices). Without that acknowledgment, the revolutionary aspect of his opinion is concealed and rendered vulnerable to the ridicule of the dissent. Far better would it have been to more closely track the superb amicus [friend of the court] briefs of the Cato Institute, which Kennedy twice cited approvingly, and of the Institute for Justice.

If the Court is serious in its ruling, Justice Scalia is right to contend that the shift from privacy to liberty, and away from the New Deal-induced tension between the presumption of constitutionality and fundamental rights, "will have far-reaching implications beyond this case." For example, the medical cannabis cases now wending their way through the Ninth Circuit would be greatly affected if those seeking to use or distribute medical cannabis pursuant to California law did not have to show that their liberty to do so was somehow "fundamental"—and instead the government were forced to justify its restrictions on that liberty. While wrongful behavior (or license) could be prohibited, rightful behavior (or liberty) could be regulated, provided that the regulation was shown to be necessary and proper.

Although it may be possible to cabin this case to the protection of "personal" liberties of an intimate nature—and it is a fair prediction that that is what the Court will attempt—for *Lawrence v. Texas* to be constitutionally revolutionary, the Court's defense of liberty must not be limited to sexual conduct. The more liberties the Court protects, the less ideological it will be and the more widespread political support it will enjoy. Recognizing a robust "presumption of liberty" might also enable the court to transcend the trench warfare over judicial appointments. Both Left and Right would then find their favored rights protected under the same doctrine. When the Court plays favorites with liberty, as it has since the New Deal, it loses rather than gains credibility with the public, and undermines its vital role as the guardian of the Constitution. If the Court is true to its reasoning, *Lawrence v. Texas* could provide an important step in the direction of a more balanced protection of liberty that could find broad ideological support.

> "Overturning the decision [Roe v. Wade]
> will breed compromise and conciliation
> in our political system instead of con-
> frontation and conflict."

The U.S. Supreme Court
Should Overturn *Roe v. Wade*

James F. Pontuso

*James F. Pontuso, a conservative commentator and author, is a
professor who teaches government and politics at Hampden-
Sydney College. In the following viewpoint, Pontuso maintains
that newly confirmed Justice Samuel Alito should vote to overturn the landmark* Roe v. Wade *decision, because it is within
the nation's long-term interests. Pontuso argues that returning
the right to decide abortion to the states would allow citizens to
have a say in this important issue, and would make the issue less
heated and divisive.*

As you read, consider the following questions:

1. What does the author believe would be Justice Samuel
   Alito's significance in overturning *Roe v. Wade*?

2. According to the author, how does James Madison describe the ideal decision-making process, which would come into play if *Roe* were overturned?

3. Why has the abortion issue become so heated, according to the author?

The current Supreme Court has avoided taking a clear stand on abortion. In 2007 the Court ruled in *Gonzales v. Carhart* that the federal government could limit "partial birth abortions" and in 2008 it refused to hear cases that had overturned state laws prohibiting women prisoners' right to abortions. In neither case did the court rule on the central issues of whether *Roe v. Wade* the 1973 case that established a woman's right to abortion.

Right to choose advocates have been concerned that Justice Samuel Alito will provide the swing vote against *Roe v. Wade*, a precedent that has been upheld in a number of 5 to 4 rulings with Sandra Day O'Connor, whose place Alito took on the Court, providing the margin of victory.

Yet, if Justice Alito's hearings before the Senate indicate his judicial temperament, it is clear that he not given to rash or bold jurisprudence. He may become convinced that overturning a long-standing precedent, especially one that has so influenced public policy as *Roe*, is an imprudent exercise of judicial authority.

If Justice Alito considers the long-term health of the nation's political institutions, however, his choice is clear. He should vote to overrule *Roe*.

There is a great deal of confusion associated with *Roe*. Many people believe that by reversing *Roe* the Supreme Court would ban abortion. But, in fact, overturning *Roe* would merely give state legislatures, governors, and ultimately the people themselves responsibility for deciding the abortion issue.

Giving voters choice on abortion would mean that the complex system of decision-making best described by James Madison and ultimately instituted in the United Sates would come into play. According to Madison partisan groups or factions must seek to convince and attract the public if they wish to have their policies adopted. If a faction becomes too adamant or confrontational, it may cause a backlash and alienate public opinion rather attract it to the cause. Blowing up buildings or intimating doctors does not garner wide-spread support.

Madison's system has served the nation well, ameliorating most of the controversial issues that have faced the country—with the exception of slavery—where the Supreme Court also interjected itself into a political dispute. Madison's scheme favors compromise and conciliation over conflict and extremism. Interested groups must endeavor to form moderate governing majorities, a task that demands convincing most people of the rightness of their policies.

It is exactly because the Court took choice over abortion away from the people that the issue has become so heated. Both sides in the abortion debate have acted irresponsibly without fear of alienating centrist voters. Pro-choice champions insist that women have an unrestricted claim to abortion and need give no thought to the duty human beings owe to one another—even to the vulnerable, such as a fetus. Pro-life adherents maintain that existence begins at conception and that women abnegate their choice in favor of the fetus's right to life, no matter how early the pregnancy. Pro-life advocates have been most adamant forwarding their position—confronting abortion clinics and threatening doctors who perform abortions—because they were on the losing side in *Roe*.

Both sides have mounted smear campaigns at nomination hearings in an effort to demonize judges whose judicial principles may lead to results with which they disagree. Senate hearings have degenerated into arenas of character assassina-

"Vietnam and Abortion Atrocities." Cartoon by Rod Rossi. www.CartoonStock.com.

tion based on rumor and innuendo. Highly qualified jurists, such as Robert Bork, have been denied appointment to the Supreme Court. Judges without distinguished records and little or no paper trail on which they can be attacked—David Souter and Clarence Thomas—have been elevated to the bench. Justice Alito's nomination was nearly sabotaged because of his distinguished, and therefore, easily discernable record. Justice Alito was most strenuously attacked by women's groups. It was more than a little ironic that the turning point of the Alito hearings came when his wife, Martha-Ann Alito—in a display of tradition gender roles—was reduced to tears by the assault on her husband's integrity.

Spokespersons for pro-choice NARAL (National Abortion and Reproductive Rights Action League) made two claims during the Alito hearings in opposition to his nominations.

First it was said that the precedent in *Roe* should be upheld—and Alito defeated—because a majority of the people now favor women's right to abortion. Second, NARAL held up the "coat hanger" image of women forced to seek illicit abortion perhaps endangering their lives.

Public opinion polls show that a majority of Americans favor some sort of legalized abortion. But if this is true, then *Roe* is no longer needed to protect women's choice since the majority, acting through elected officials, can legislate to sustain that right. Moreover, the same shift in opinion that supports abortion is evident in the public's attitude toward unwed mothers. The shame of bearing a child out of wedlock has immeasurably lessoned, if not disappeared completely. This shift is evident in the public attitude toward Hollywood celebrities whose careers have not been hurt by parenting children without benefit of marriage. Absent the social stigma, it is unlikely that many women will risk their lives to obtain illicit abortions.

If responsibility for abortion policy is returned to state legislatures, women in some states will lose the freedom to terminate unwanted pregnancies. Conservative states such as Utah may ban all abortions. Of course, women could seek abortions in states more hospitable to their right to choose. Moreover, Congress could mandate equal treatment either through a general law or by withholding federal dollars, say Medicaid funds, to those states that do not follow its guidelines. Democrats could even use the abortion issue to sustain their majority in Congress if, as NARAL suggests, the public favors the right to choose.

In most states, the legislative process will mostly likely establish laws that recognize women's rights to control their own bodies, but place some restrictions on those rights as the fetus develops. It is unlikely that purists on either side will be happy with this solution. But it is the strength of Madison's scheme to create temperate solutions to volatile problems, ones that are acceptable to the moderate center and not extreme factions.

Justice Alito should cast his vote against the precedent in *Roe*. Overturning the decision will breed compromise and conciliation in our political system instead of confrontation and conflict. It will go a long way to bringing back civility to Supreme Court nomination hearings and may insure that future judges tapped for the highest court will not have to endure the humiliating spectacle that he did.

"*In rejecting* Roe, *and in attempting to eliminate the right of privacy, fundamentalists are attacking many decades of American law.*"

The U.S. Supreme Court Should Not Overturn *Roe v. Wade*

Cass Sunstein

Cass Sunstein is a legal scholar specializing in constitutional law. In 2009 he became the head of the White House Office of Information and Regulatory Affairs. In the following viewpoint, Sunstein argues that although there are a number of flaws in the 1973 Roe v. Wade *decision, it should not be overturned. Sunstein writes that respect for established precedent is vital to our judicial system and* Roe v. Wade *should stand.*

As you read, consider the following questions:

1. What is the first irony regarding the *Roe v. Wade* decision, according to the author?

2. Why does the author believe *Roe* was decided poorly?

3. What does Justice Ruth Bader Ginsburg think of the *Roe* decision?

The ruling in *Roe [v. Wade]*, one of the most controversial in the nation's entire history, has long dominated debates over the future direction of the Supreme Court. In every recent presidential election, the question, *What will be the future of the Supreme Court?* is often taken, by liberals and conservatives alike, to be code for, *What will happen to the right to choose abortion?* Among liberals, preservation of *Roe* has probably been the most pressing issue in thinking about Supreme Court appointments. In recent years, conservatives have been a bit quieter. But for many of them, overruling *Roe* has been a high priority. There is no question that legal fundamentalists have long had *Roe* in their sights—and that in many ways it stands as the fundamentalists' Public Enemy Number One.

As a political matter, there are three major ironies here, and they are all relevant to thinking about the role of the Supreme Court in American life. The first irony: *Roe* was decided in 1973, at a time when the nation was rapidly moving in the direction of easing up restrictions on abortion. The society's moral trend-line was clear. For better or for worse, it was pro-choice, not pro-life. In 1973, the Court seemed to be ratifying a trend that was well underway. But in a few years, the Court's decision helped to create the pro-life movement—and thus gave a lot of new energy and organization to people who had been relatively quiet on the abortion question. In short, the Court fueled its own opposition. (Perfectionists and liberal activists take note.)

The second irony: *Roe* is a crucial decision for women's groups, many of whose members have long seen the ruling as central to women's equality. But from the standpoint of equality, the Court's decision has been a mixed blessing. The decision in *Roe* almost certainly contributed to the defeat of the Equal Rights Amendment. It also helped to demobilize the women's movement and at the same time to activate the strongest opponents of that movement.

The third irony: Democrats have made preservation of *Roe* a central issue in presidential elections, and many Republican leaders have made it clear that they would like the Court to overrule the decision. But if *Roe* were overruled, Democrats would almost certainly be helped and Republicans would almost certainly be hurt. Everyone knows that if abortion really becomes an active issue again—if abortion might actually be a crime—then countless Americans will vote for pro-choice candidates. A judicial decision to overrule *Roe* would immediately create a major crisis for the Republican Party. Some red states would undoubtedly turn blue or at least purple.

Choice Then and Choice Now

But my topic here is law, not politics. To understand the constitutional issue, we have to distinguish between two questions. The first is whether the Court should have done what it did in 1973. The second is what the Court should do now.

Minimalists are greatly embarrassed by *Roe*, and rightly so. This was the Court's first encounter with the abortion question, and the Court badly overreached, deciding many issues unnecessarily. Not only did the Court announce a broad right to choose abortion; it also developed a complex and rigid trimester system, in which it specified what states may do in each three-month period of a pregnancy. By saying so much, the Court ignored the minimalists' most fervent plea: In the most controversial cases, judges should proceed narrowly rather than broadly. With its ambitious ruling, not at all firmly rooted in precedent, the Court allowed pro-life citizens to think that they had been treated with contempt—as if their own moral commitments could be simply brushed aside by federal judges.

Perhaps the Court's ambitious ruling in *Roe* could be justified if the Constitution plainly banned states from outlawing

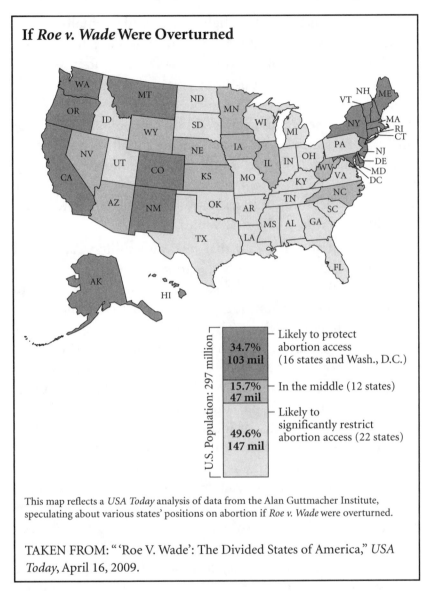

If *Roe v. Wade* Were Overturned

U.S. Population: 297 million

34.7%
103 mil — Likely to protect abortion access (16 states and Wash., D.C.)

15.7%
47 mil — In the middle (12 states)

49.6%
147 mil — Likely to significantly restrict abortion access (22 states)

This map reflects a *USA Today* analysis of data from the Alan Guttmacher Institute, speculating about various states' positions on abortion if *Roe v. Wade* were overturned.

TAKEN FROM: " 'Roe V. Wade': The Divided States of America," *USA Today*, April 16, 2009.

abortion. But the Constitution does not plainly do that. Even if the Due Process Clause recognizes a right to privacy, many people think that the protection of fetal life is extremely important. As a matter of constitutional law, protecting fetal life may well be a constitutionally sufficient reason to intrude on the right to choose.

It is no wonder, in this light, that fundamentalists want the Court to overrule *Roe v. Wade* and to allow states to regulate abortion as they like. Justice Scalia's words nicely summarize the fundamentalist position: "We should get out of this area, where we have no right to be, and where we do neither ourselves nor the country any good by remaining." In fact *Roe* can easily be seen as a case study in the pitfalls of perfectionism. Not only did the [decision] split the country; it also ignored one of the most remarkable virtues of a federal system, which is to allow different resolutions in different states, with their different mixes of moral values.

It is not at all silly to say that *Roe* was simply wrong—that the Court would have done better to stay out of the abortion controversy. But there is a reasonable alternative position. In dealing with the abortion question, the Court could have proceeded much more slowly. The Texas law challenged in *Roe* was exceedingly severe. It banned abortion even in cases in which the mother would face serious health problems from bringing the child to term, even in cases in which the pregnancy resulted from rape, and even in cases in which the pregnancy was a product of incest. The Court could have emphasized these points so as to rule quite narrowly. It could have said that even if states may protect fetal life, they may not require women to carry children to term when they have been raped and when childbirth would seriously endanger their health. The Court also dealt, in *Roe*, with a Georgia law that created a host of peculiar obstacles and burdens, going far beyond what was necessary to protect the state's legitimate interests. The Court might have struck down severe restrictions of this kind without deciding the most controversial questions about how to balance the rights of women and the protection of fetal life.

Justice Ruth Bader Ginsburg is one of the leading advocates for women's equality in the history of American law. But she is also a minimalist. She has herself argued that *Roe v.*

Wade was a mistake, simply because it overreached—and that the Court would have done much better if it had proceeded in a narrow fashion. One of the major advantages of this way of proceeding is that the Court would not have dictated a solution of its own. It would have participated in a dialogue about the abortion question, listening to what other institutions, and citizens, had to say.

What about *Roe* today? Fundamentalists insist that *Roe* was wrong and should be immediately overruled. But it is not senseless to think that, although *Roe* was wrong, and a big mistake, the Court should not now overrule it. Much of constitutional law is built on decisions with which current judges disagree. Our system works because it is based on respect for precedent; if judges overruled precedents simply because they disagree with them, constitutional law would be hopelessly unstable. Many fundamentalists believe that in constitutional law, judges should not much respect precedent. But this is arrogant. To be sure, precedents are not set in stone; the Court has overruled many of its decisions, including those permitting segregation and invalidating maximum-hour and minimum-wage laws. But when a decision has become an established part of American life, judges should have a strong presumption in its favor. Minimalists do not like radical shifts, and overruling *Roe* would certainly count as that.

Minimalists are willing to agree that the Constitution permits reasonable restrictions on the right to choose abortion. If states want to ensure that the choice of abortion is adequately informed, or to require a serious consultation with doctors before abortions are chosen, the Constitution should not stand in the way. Minimalists think that the Court might well have been wrong to forbid bans on what is sometimes called "partial birth abortion." Most important, minimalists respect *Roe's* critics. They agree that *Roe* has shaky constitutional foundations. They know that countless citizens of good faith believe that abortion is a morally troublesome act; many minimalists share that belief. As a matter of constitutional law, minimalists are far from sure that *Roe* was right. But they are willing to accept it, not in spite of but because of their essential conservatism.

In rejecting *Roe*, and in attempting to eliminate the right of privacy, fundamentalists are attacking many decades of American law. That kind of attack is entirely characteristic of the fundamentalist program.

> *"The time has come for the nation's po-*
> *litical left to remind voters that so*
> *many of the rights and privileges that*
> *people enjoy today were established*
> *more than a generation ago by a Su-*
> *preme Court that viewed the Constitu-*
> *tion as a tool for expanding and de-*
> *fending human dignity and indepen-*
> *dence."*

The U.S. Supreme Court Should Limit the Role of Religion in Public Life

Frederick S. Lane

Frederick S. Lane is an author and a professor at Bernard M. Baruch College, the City University of New York. In the follow-ing viewpoint, Lane predicts how the current U.S. Supreme Court led by Justice John Roberts would rule on a variety of is-sues regarding the separation of church and state. Lane notes the Christian right has had significant success in reshaping the ideol-ogy of the Supreme Court in the past several decades and if lib-

erals want to ensure fundamental rights of religious freedom and privacy they must remind voters of the importance of such values.

As you read, consider the following questions:

1. What is the *Lemon* test, as described by the author?

2. How does the author predict the current U.S. Supreme Court will rule on the issue of displaying the Ten Commandments in public buildings?

3. Why would the "religious right" view the retirement of Justice Sandra Day O'Connor as a loss, according to the author?

While keeping in mind that there are no guarantees as to how the members of the [U.S. Supreme] Court will vote on a particular issue (as the Religious Right is painfully aware), there are some predictions that can be made about how the relatively [2005] new [Chief Justice John] Roberts Court might decide various religious issues, and what might happen in the future.

The *Lemon* Test

It is difficult to hold out much hope for the continued viability of the *Lemon* test, the current standard for evaluating whether a particular government program or action violates the principle of separation of church and state. With increasing frequency, conservative members of the Court have shown a willingness to simply ignore the *Lemon* test, or have narrowly construed it to the point of insignificance. The Roberts Court may formally abandon it altogether.

The replacement of William Rehnquist with John Roberts is not likely to make much difference in the Court's actual voting pattern, but it is worth remembering that Roberts worked on the solicitor general's brief in *Lee v. Weisman*, in which the elder [George H.W.] Bush administration asked the Court to abandon the test altogether. Of much greater potential significance is the replacement of Sandra Day O'Connor with the presumably more consistent Samuel Alito. On issue after issue, Alito may tip the Court in a more conservative direction.

In *Lee*, for instance, O'Connor joined the majority opinion drafted by Anthony Kennedy. If Alito had been serving instead, it seems likely that the majority opinion would have been written by Justice [Antonin] Scalia, thereby abandoning *Lemon* and upholding prayer during school graduation ceremonies. Far more importantly, it is likely that Scalia would have used the case to announce a much narrower church-state test, one that would find "establishment of religion" by a government program only when there was financial support for religion *and* the threat of penalty for noncompliance or nonadherence (such as jail time for not attending church). To put it mildly, Scalia's approach would eviscerate contemporary boundaries between church and state.

The Ten Commandments

The church and state issue on which the Court seems the most divided is the publicly supported display of the Ten Commandments. . . . In 2005 the Supreme Court simultaneously issued two contradictory 5-4 decisions involving different types of Decalogue displays: in *Van Orden v. Perry* the Court voted to uphold the constitutionality of a stone monument on the state capitol in Texas, but in *McCreary County v. ACLU of Kentucky* it struck down a Kentucky law requiring the courthouse display of the Ten Commandments.

Given the narrow margins and the struggles by the lower courts to interpret and apply the Court's decisions, it seems likely that the Court will take up the issue again in the near future. One entertaining possibility is the *Summum v. Pleasant Grove City* case, in which a relatively new religion is suing to have its pyramid-shaped monument, inscribed with its Seven Aphorisms, displayed next to the city's Ten Commandments monument. The American Center for Law and Justice, the legal foundation established by *700 Club* televangelist Pat Robertson, is actively soliciting funds to help take the case to the Supreme Court on behalf of the city.

If a new Ten Commandments case reaches the Supreme Court, it is likely to get a sympathetic hearing. Justice O'Connor voted against the constitutionality of the Ten Commandments display in both *Van Orden* and *McCreary*. If both Chief Justice Roberts and Justice Alito align themselves with the existing conservative bloc of the Court, they could arguably legalize the publicly supported display of the Ten Commandments in every public building in the country.

Public-Supported Holiday Displays

The issues surrounding holiday displays . . . seem more settled. Admittedly, the decision in *Allegheny County v. Greater Pittsburgh ACLU* is hardly an example of doctrinal clarity, given the number of separate opinions written by the Court, but the justices have not shown any interest in revisiting the issue in nearly twenty years. However, it is important to remember that four members of the *Allegheny County* Court (Chief Justice Rehnquist and Justices [Byron] White, Scalia, and Kennedy) voted to uphold the constitutionality of Pittsburgh's Nativity display, notwithstanding its prominent placement in a government building, its lack of secular elements, and its overtly sectarian message. . . .

Prayer and Evolution in the Public Schools

The Court decided *Wallace v. Jaffree*, the case that struck down the Alabama law providing for a moment of silence "for meditation or silent prayer," more than twenty years ago. It seems unlikely, even given the personnel changes that have occurred since then, that the Court will revisit the issue of prayer in the classroom.

A more likely candidate for reconsideration is the issue of prayer at school graduations or other events, such as football games. The *Lee v. Weisman* case, which invalidated the practice of prayer in graduation ceremonies, was a 5-4 decision made narrower by the fact that Justice Kennedy switched sides during the deliberations. The margin on the football-game prayer decision, *Santa Independent School District v. Doe*, was slightly larger (6-3), but hardly unassailable. In both cases, Justice O'Connor joined the majority in invalidating the challenged governmental practices. Should the Court reverse one or both of those decisions, then not only will the practice of prayer become far more prevalent at school functions, but the Court would inevitably be entangled in doctrinal battles over how such prayers may be phrased and delivered. The Court has enough of a challenge conducting the constitutional parsing for which it is trained; it would be particularly ill-suited to the task of splitting theological hairs. More importantly, such debates by their very nature will shatter the concept of separation of church and state.

As for the Christian Right's repeated efforts to water down the teaching of evolution, the chances seem low that the Roberts Court will take up the issue in the near future. The Court's ruling twenty years ago in *Edwards v. Aguillard* . . . firmly (7-2) rejected the parallel teaching of "creation science," and the 2005 U.S. District Court decision in *Kitzmiller v. Dover Area School District* appears to have substantially slowed the push to get public schools to incorporate "intelligent design" into their curricula.

Religion in the Workplace

The Court's position regarding the role of religion in the workplace . . . is somewhat less ideologically consistent than other church-state issues. When the Court ruled in *Employment Div., Ore. Dept. of Human Resources v. Smith* that employees could not claim a "free exercise" exception to a generally applicable criminal law, the 6-3 majority consisted of justices from the Court's left, right, and center voting blocs. Only the Court's most liberal justices (William Brennan, Harry Blackmun, and Thurgood Marshall) dissented.

When Congress tried to reverse the *Smith* decision legislatively, by passing the Religious Freedom Restoration Act, a similar 6-3 majority (equally mixed ideologically) struck down the law as it applied to state legislation in *City of Boerne v. Flores*. Justice O'Connor (along with Justices [David] Souter and [Stephen] Breyer) dissented in *Boerne*, arguing that the Court had erred in *Smith* by making it easier for a government to justify a "substantial burden" on a religious practice.

The Religious Right usually does not have much positive to say about Justice O'Connor, but in this one area, at least, the movement may see her departure as a loss. In balancing the religious rights of the individual versus the police power of the state, O'Connor made it clear that the state should be required to show both a compelling state interest and a narrowly tailored approach. That is not a view likely to be endorsed by her replacement, Justice Alito.

The Right to Privacy

Forty years after the Supreme Court first recognized a "right to privacy," the legal doctrine seems firmly and securely established. . . . Every member of the current Supreme Court (aside from Justice [John Paul] Stevens) has publicly stated that he or she believes that the Constitution contains such a right, even though neither the phrase nor even the word "privacy" appears in the Constitution. Absent the unlikely appointment of a justice with views as legally rigid as Robert Bork, there is little likelihood that the Court will flatly overturn the right to privacy that evolved from the *Griswold* and *Eisenstadt* cases. Only in the Christian Right's most salacious dreams would state government regain the ability to dictate a couple's birth control choices, for instance, or once again jail someone for fornication (the crime of sex between unmarried individuals).

But in 2007 . . . in *Gonzales v. Carhart,* five justices (Scalia, Kennedy, [Clarence] Thomas, Roberts, and Alito) for the first time since *Roe v. Wade,* upheld a law that places limitations on a woman's decision to have a previability abortion [an abortion prior to the time when a fetus could survive on its own outside the womb], a period of time which the Court had previously said was exclusively within a woman's zone of privacy. It is worth noting that the only opinion that even mentioned the term "privacy" was Justice [Ruth Bader] Ginsburg's impassioned dissent, which was joined by Justices Stevens, Souter, and Breyer. And as Ginsburg pointed out, the challenge to the "undue restriction" imposed by the Partial-Birth Abortion Ban was not an attempt "to vindicate some generalized notion of privacy; rather, [it centers] on a woman's autonomy to determine her life's course, and thus to enjoy equal citizenship stature."

The fact that a majority of the Court was willing to endorse an infringement on a woman's right to privacy without even discussing the concept or using the word does not bode well for the full preservation of the citizenship stature of women in the future. Equally disturbing is the Court's willingness to defer to congressional findings that were repeatedly and conclusively shown to be false or at best misleading. And as Justice Ginsburg noted, the language used by the Court's majority opinion reveals a "hostility to the right *Roe* and *Casey* secured." There is good reason to worry that even while the Roberts Court in this or future iterations will not go so far as to abandon the right to privacy altogether, the Court will be increasingly receptive to greater and greater intrusions on a woman's right of privacy and self-determination.

A Forgotten and Threatened Court

Since the 1970s, in the wake of [evangelical Christian] Francis Schaeffer's call to arms, the Religious Right has viewed the composition of the Supreme Court as a political problem, and

Christian conservatives have aggressively used the tools of politics to try to solve the problem. If Americans who value such fundamental principles as separation of church and state and personal privacy do not do the same, they may be stunned by the rapidity with which those values are severely diminished or eliminated altogether.

More than anything else, the relative success of the Religious Right in reshaping the Supreme Court—and there is no question that it has done so—has stemmed from the fact that all too many people take the decisions of the [Earl] Warren Court for granted. More than any other single interest group, the Christian Right has educated its supporters on the connection between political success and judicial change, and it has consistently and aggressively worked for the appointment of federal judges and Supreme Court justices who share its philosophical opposition to the Warren Court's rulings. The time has come for the nation's political left to remind voters that so many of the rights and privileges that people enjoy today were established more than a generation ago by a Supreme Court that viewed the Constitution as a tool for expanding and defending human dignity and independence.

If that education does not take place, much of what the remarkable Warren Court accomplished will be weakened or wiped out by a social and political movement that more than anything else wants to baptize the United States as a Christian nation and use the Bible as its primary source of legal authority. In the end, the goal of the Religious Right is nothing less than to bring this country to its knees.

> *"The Court has brought law and religion into opposition. The results are damaging to both fields."*

The U.S. Supreme Court Should Not Limit the Role of Religion in Public Life

Robert Bork

Robert Bork is a conservative jurist, legal scholar, and author. In the following viewpoint, Bork asserts that the liberal intelligentsia has succeeded in spreading antagonism toward religion to the U.S. judiciary. Bork traces the Supreme Court decisions that allowed the Court to marginalize the role of religion in public life and he concludes that when law becomes antagonistic to religion, it is undermining the greater moral good needed for civilized societies.

As you read, consider the following questions:

1. How does the author believe the Supreme Court decision in *Flast v. Cohen* illustrates the Court's attitude toward religion?

2. According to the author, how does the *Lemon* test erase all hints of religion in government domains?

3. Why does the author believe *Lee v. Weisman* was decided wrongly?

The liberal intelligentsia is overwhelmingly secular and fearful of religion; hence its incessant harping on the dangers posed by the "religious right." That ominous phrase is intended to suggest that Americans who are conservative and religious are a threat to the Republic, for they are probably intending to establish a theocracy and to institute an ecumenical version of the Inquisition. (Exasperated, a friend suggested that the press should begin referring to the "pagan left.") It is certainly true, however, that the liberal intelligentsia's antagonism to religion is now a prominent feature of American jurisprudence. The Court moved rather suddenly from tolerance of religion and religious expression to fierce hostility.

Flast v. Cohen

Though not the first manifestation, one case illustrates the place of religion on the Court's scale of values. Major philosophical shifts in the law sometimes occur through what may seem to laymen mere tinkerings with technical doctrine. The judiciary's power to marginalize religion in public life was vastly increased through a change in the law of what lawyers call "standing," which withholds the power to litigate from persons claiming only a generalized or ideological interest in an issue. Some direct impact on the plaintiff, such as the loss of money or liberty, is required. But in 1968, in *Flast v. Cohen*, the Supreme Court created the entirely novel rule that taxpayers can sue under the establishment clause to prohibit federal expenditures aiding religious schools. The Court refused to allow similar suits to be brought under other parts of the Constitution. Thus, every single provision of the Constitution, from Article I, section 1, to the Twenty-Seventh Amendment, except one, is immune from taxpayer or citizen enforcement—and that exception is the one used to attack public manifestations of religion.

Now we are treated to the preposterous spectacle of lawsuits by persons whose only complaint is that they are "offended" by seeing a religious symbol, such as a creche or a menorah, on public property during a holiday season or even by the sight of the Ten Commandments on a plaque on a high school wall. Apparently those who do not like religion are exquisitely sensitive to the pain of being reminded of it, but the religious are assumed to have no right to such feelings about the banishment of religion from the public arena.

The *Lemon* Test

The distance between the Court's position on religion and the Framers' and ratifiers' understanding of the First Amendment was revealed, though not for the first time, in *Lemon v. Kurtzman*. The case created a three-part test that, if applied consistently, would erase all hints of religion in any public context. In order to survive judicial scrutiny a statute or practice must have a secular legislative purpose; its principal or primary effect must be one that neither advances nor inhibits religion; and it must not foster an excessive government entanglement with religion. Few statutes or governmental practices that brush anywhere in the vicinity of religion can pass all those tests.

Yet the Supreme Court narrowly approved Nebraska's employment of a chaplain for its legislature in *Marsh v. Chambers*. Though the dissent correctly pointed out that the *Lemon* test was violated, as it was in each of its three criteria, the majority relied on the fact that employing chaplains to open legislative sessions with prayers conformed to historic precedent: Not only did the Continental Congress employ a chaplain but so did both houses of the first Congress, which also proposed the First Amendment. That same Congress also provided paid

Religion and Views of Christmas Displays

Christmas displays on govt. property should be...	Total	White Evang.	White Mainline	White Catholic	Secular
	%	%	%	%	%
Allowed	83	95	83	91	63
Only with other symbols too	27	28	24	37	23
Even if displayed alone	44	59	49	44	27
Doesn't matter/DK/Ref	12	8	10	10	13
Not allowed	11	2	12	6	25
Doesn't matter/don't care (vol.)	4	1	4	1	9
Don't know (vol.)	2	2	1	2	3
	100	100	100	100	100

TAKEN FROM: Pew Research Center for the People & Press, 2005.

chaplains for the Army and the Navy. The Court often pays little attention to the historic meaning of the Constitution, but it would be particularly egregious to hold that those who sent the amendment to the states for ratification intended to prohibit what they had just done themselves. That *Lemon* fails when specific historical evidence is available necessarily means that, in cases where specific history is not discoverable, *Lemon* destroys laws and practices that were meant to be allowable.

There is no lack of other evidence to show that no absolute barrier to any interaction between government and religion was intended. From the beginning of the Republic, Congress called upon presidents to issue Thanksgiving Day proclamations in the name of God. All the presidents complied, with the sole exception of Jefferson, who thought such proclamations at odds with the principle of the establishment clause. Jefferson's tossed-off metaphor in a letter about the "wall" between church and state has become the modern law, despite the fact that it was idiosyncratic and not at all what Congress and the ratifying states understood themselves to be saying. The first Congress readopted the Northwest Ordinance, initially passed by the Continental Congress, which stated that "religion, morality, and knowledge, being necessary to good government and the happiness of mankind, schools and the means of learning shall forever be encouraged." The ordinance required that specified amounts of land be set aside for churches.

Schools and Prayer

Yet in *Lee v. Weisman*, a six-justice majority held that a short, bland, non-sectarian prayer at a public school commencement amounted to an establishment of religion. The Court saw government interference with religion in the very fact that the school principal asked the rabbi to offer a nonsectarian prayer. Coercion of Deborah Weisman was detected in the possibility that she might feel "peer pressure" to stand or at least to maintain respectful silence during the prayer. She would, of course, have had no constitutional case had the commencement speaker read from *The Communist Manifesto* or *Mein Kampf* while peer pressure and school authorities required her to maintain a respectful silence. Only religion is beyond the judge-erected pale. In this way a long tradition across the entire nation of prayer at public school graduation ceremonies came to an end.

One more example will suffice. In *Santa Fe Independent School Dist. v. Doe*, the school district arranged student elections to determine whether invocations should be delivered before high school football games and, if so, to select students to deliver them. The student could make a statement or read a nonsectarian, nonproselytizing prayer. The Supreme Court majority held that "school sponsorship of a religious message is impermissible because it sends the ancillary message to members of the audience who are nonadherents 'that they are outsiders, not full members of the political community, and an accompanying message to adherents that they are insiders, favored members of the political community.'" The nonadherent was put to "the choice between whether to attend these games or to risk facing a personally offensive religious ritual." The incredibly thin skin of nonadherents is constitutional dogma. The Court repeatedly referred to the elections as "majoritarian," as though that made them all the more threatening. The opinion is remarkable for a tone that "bristles with hostility to all things religious in public life," Chief William H. Justice Rehnquist noted in dissent. The majority opinion, it might be said, also bristles with hostility to majoritarian (i.e., democratic) processes. Still more remarkable, and sadly ironic, is the majority's statement that "one of the purposes served by the Establishment Clause is to remove debate over this kind of issue from governmental supervision or control." That is precisely what the decision does not do. The Court's pronounced antireligious animus [feeling of ill will], displayed in decades of decisions, has itself produced angry debate that is under the control of the Supreme Court, a branch of government.

At some point, parody is the only appropriate response. Nude dancing is entitled to considerable protection as "expressive" behavior, according to *Erie v. Pap's A.M.* Theodore Olson, a leading Supreme Court advocate and [from 2001 to 2004] solicitor general of the United States, was prompted to suggest that high school students should dance nude before football games because naked dancing is preferred to prayer as a form of expression. He might have noted, of course, that nudity must not be achieved through the Dance of the Seven Veils because that has biblical connotations!

Courts Have Gone Too Far

Lower courts have found a forbidden "establishment of religion" in the most innocuous practices: a high school football team praying for an injury-free game; a local ordinance forbidding the sale of nonkosher foods as kosher; a small child trying to read a child's version of a religious story before a class; a teacher reading the Bible silently during a reading period (because students, who did not know what the teacher was reading, might, if they found out, be influenced by his choice of reading material). The Court's establishment clause decisions show the same devotion to radical individual autonomy as do the speech cases. The words "Congress shall make no law respecting an establishment of religion" might have been read, as common understanding would suggest, merely to preclude government recognition of an official church or to prohibit discriminatory aid to one or a few religions. No one reading the establishment clause when it was ratified in 1791 could have anticipated the unhistorical sweep it would develop under the sway of modern liberalism to produce, as [Catholic priest and founder of the neoconservative group Institute on Religion and Public Life] Richard John Neuhaus put it, a "public square naked of religious symbol and substance."

The Court has brought law and religion into opposition. The results are damaging to both fields. All law rests upon choices guided by moral assumptions and beliefs. There is no reason to prohibit any conduct, except on the understanding that some moral good is thereby served. Though the proposition is certainly not undisputed, an excellent case can be made that religion, though not the original source of moral understanding, is an indispensable reinforcement of that understanding. It is surely significant that, as religious belief has declined, moral behavior has worsened as well. When law becomes antagonistic to religion, it undermines its own main support.

Christopher Lasch [social critic and historian], who was by no means a conservative, asked: "What accounts for [our society's] wholesale defection from the standards of personal conduct—civility, industry, self-restraint—that were once considered indispensable to democracy?" He answered that a major reason is the "gradual decay of religion." Our liberal elites, whose "attitude to religion," Lasch said, "ranges from indifference to active hostility," have succeeded in removing religion from public recognition and debate. Indeed, it could be added that the Court has almost succeeded in establishing a new religion: secular humanism. That is what the intelligentsia want, it is what they are getting, and we may all be the worse for it.

Periodical Bibliography

The following articles have been selected to supplement the diverse views presented in this chapter.

Cynthia Gorney   "Law and Revulsion," *American Prospect*, April 27, 2007. www.prospect.org/cs/ articles?article=law_and_revulsion.

Heather Gray   "The Supreme Court Looks a Lot Like the Taliban," *CounterPunch*, April 20, 2007. www.counterpunch.org/gray04202007.html.

Michael Kinsley   "What Abortion Debate?" *Washington Post*, November 18, 2005. www.washingtonpost.com/ wp-dyn/content/article/2005/11/17/ AR2005111701452.html.

David L. Kirp   "Racists and Robber Barons," *Nation*, July 30, 2007. www.thenation.com/doc/20070730/kirp.

John Nichols   "The Politics of Supreme Court Nominations," *Nation* Blogs, April 18, 2007. www.thenation.com/blogs/state_of_change/ 187372.

Roger Pilon   "Alito and Abortion," *Wall Street Journal*, November 28, 2005.

Katha Pollitt   "Regrets Only," *Nation*, April 26, 2007. www.thenation.com/doc/20070514/pollitt.

David T. Pyne   "Bush Moves the Supreme Court to the Left," *IntellectualConservative.com*, October 17, 2005. www.intellectualconservative.com/2005/10/17/ bush-moves-the-supreme-court-to-the-left-2/.

Rick Santorum   "The Constitutional Wrecking Ball," *National Review Online*, July 19, 2005. www.nationalreview.com/comment/ santorum200507190728.asp.

Michael P. Tremoglie   "Theophobia: Part One," *IntellectualConservative.com*, January 10, 2005.

OPPOSING
VIEWPOINTS®
SERIES

CHAPTER 3

What Factors Should Be Considered for U.S. Supreme Court Nominees?

Chapter Preface

O n July 1, 1987, conservative judge and legal scholar Robert Bork was nominated by President Ronald Reagan to the U.S. Supreme Court. Bork certainly had the credentials to assume a position on the Court: he had served as solicitor general in the U.S. Department of Justice; he had been a circuit judge for the U.S. Court of Appeals for eight years; and he had written a number of books on legal issues. So when moderate Justice Lewis Powell announced his retirement, President Reagan confidently chose Bork to replace him. What followed, however, was one of the most controversial and hard-fought nomination battles in recent U.S. Supreme Court history.

Alarmed by the Court's potential swing to the political right that Bork's nomination represented, Democrats in the Senate immediately mobilized to oppose him. They argued he was a right-wing ideologue whose partisan decisions would destroy years of judicial precedent. Senators such as Edward Kennedy and Joe Biden asserted that Bork might vote to overrule landmark decisions on abortion, civil rights, and the separation between church and state. Civil rights and women's groups poured millions of dollars into advertisements in hopes of building opposition to Bork's nomination.

Conservative supporters of the nomination countered by claiming that Bork was actually a centrist judge that would decide cases with an open mind and sound legal reasoning. President Reagan and other conservatives defended Bork strongly, and conservative groups mounted expensive public-relations campaigns of their own to defend the Bork nomination.

Even before Bork's confirmation hearings began, Democratic senators signaled they would be asking tough questions—including how Bork would decide on a number of controversial issues, such as *Roe v. Wade* and the role of religion in government domains. Bork gave blunt answers to the Senate Judiciary Committee on how he would vote and the legal reasoning behind it. In particular, his criticism of *Roe v. Wade* generated much attention from the press and from liberal and conservative groups. On October 23, 1987, the Senate rejected Bork's nomination to the Supreme Court.

With the rejection of Bork, judicial commentators noted the process had become intensely partisan and subject to political maneuvering. As such, future nominees were advised to be less blunt and open about their political ideology and judicial leanings. Potential justices were coached to give vague responses or to reveal little information during questioning. It was thought that in this way, nominees could draw less partisan ire than Bork had and therefore have a better chance of being confirmed by the Senate.

Robert Bork's contested confirmation hearings have profoundly influenced the judicial nomination process. The following chapter presents viewpoints that explore aspects of that process, such as whether a nominee's political and religious views should be a litmus test for confirmation and whether a nominee should answer questions on how he or she would decide cases.

> "Provided that they are careful to avoid
> . . . excesses the members of the Senate
> [in U.S. Supreme Court confirmation
> hearings] are not only entitled to con-
> sider ideology as the president has done,
> they have a responsibility to do so."

Political Ideology Is Relevant in U.S. Supreme Court Confirmation Hearings

Center for American Progress Contributor

The Center for American Progress (CAP) is a liberal think tank and advocacy organization. In the following viewpoint, the group underscores the important role the U.S. Supreme Court plays in deciding a number of controversial and wide-ranging issues, such as abortion, voting rights, environmental protection, and the separation of church and state. CAP argues it is essential for senators to evaluate carefully the ideology of all Supreme Court nominees to ensure only individuals who will protect fundamental rights and who are within the constitutional mainstream are confirmed.

Center for American Progress Contributor, "Ideology Matters," *Center for American Progress*, 2004, pp. 235–238, 242. Copyright © Center for American Progress. This material was created by the Center for American Progress, www.americanprogress.org.

As you read, consider the following questions:

1. How does CAP define the term "ideology" in relation to nominations to the U.S. Supreme Court?

2. According to CAP, senators should object to nominees who hold what kind of views?

3. What has Charles Schumer said about the role of ideology in the confirmation process?

Over the next four years [2004–2008], President Bush will almost certainly have the opportunity to nominate one or more justices to the Supreme Court of the United States and a substantial number of additional judges to the lower federal courts. His choices will have a profound influence on the course of American society for decades to come.

As the ultimate interpreters of the Constitution, the federal courts play a central role in such sharply contested issues as abortion, voting rights, property rights, environmental protection, privacy, religious expression, the death penalty, the rights of criminal defendants and the financing of political campaigns. These issues will continue to dominate the courts' agendas in the coming years.

The judges who decide these questions should have the character, training, life experience, and breadth of understanding to appreciate the meaning and significance of the cases that come before them, both for the litigants and for society, and to make difficult choices among competing legal principles and social goods. Their decisions will also invariably reflect what is commonly referred to as their "ideology"—their beliefs about the Constitution and the role of the courts in interpreting it; their substantive views on the law; and the philosophical ideas and attitudes that inform their worldview. It is for this reason that it is important for the Senate to evaluate carefully the ideology of all judicial nominees to ensure that only individuals who operate within the constitutional mainstream and are committed to the protection of fundamental rights are confirmed to lifetime appointments on the federal bench.

The importance of ideology in judicial decisionmaking is apparent from an examination of the line of decisions in which the courts have construed the scope of congressional power to enact national policies to protect civil rights and safeguard the citizenry against such threats as those posed by terrorism, lawlessness, and corporate irresponsibility. For the past quarter century, that authority has been under assault. The Supreme Court and the lower federal courts have become increasingly dominated by ultraconservative and "activist" judges who, far from deferring to the political branches, as they claim to do, have taken a restrictive view of Congress's powers to regulate under the Commerce Clause and to enforce the Equal Protection and Due Process Clauses of the Fourteenth Amendment.

In a series of 5-4 decisions, the Rehnquist Court has struck down more laws than any court in modern history, invalidating statutes that: prohibited the carrying of guns near school grounds; required local police officers to carry out criminal background checks on gun purchasers; permitted state employees to challenge discrimination based on age and disability; and permitted victims of sexual assault to sue their attackers. Nor has the Court hesitated to strike down measures embraced by conservatives as well as progressives, such as the Religious Freedom Restoration Act, which mandated strict review of governmental actions that burden religious exercise.

In light of these cases, it is surprising to hear it argued on the right that judges should simply "apply the law" and not second-guess the legislature; that ideology does not determine how judges decide particular cases, and therefore ideological considerations should play no role in the judicial selection process. Although many cases are decided on established law and precedent, it is clear that in many important and closely contested cases, a judge's ideology plays a significant and often decisive role.

Thirty-four percent of the cases reported by the Supreme Court last term were decided by a 5-4 or 6-3 margin, and most of these decisions divided along recognizably conservative/progressive lines. While not all Republican appointees have proven as reliably right-wing as progressives feared—or as the presidents who selected them might have wished—the rightward shift in the composition of the federal bench has resulted in a lack of balance and an increasingly narrow range of viewpoints.

Having done so much to accelerate this shift during his first administration, President [George W.] Bush shows little inclination to correct it during his second. It is therefore essential that senators vigorously exercise their constitutional authority to give or withhold their "Advice and Consent" to judicial nominations. They should carefully evaluate the fitness of the president's nominees, confirming only those who recognize that the meaning of the Constitution has continued to evolve to meet the needs of a changing society, are committed to protecting fundamental constitutional rights, and will consider each case with an open mind. Senators should object strenuously to any nominee whose views on the Constitution and the judicial function are antagonistic to due process, the right to privacy, and equal protection of the laws. And they should oppose those whose ideology is inimical to congressional efforts to defend these fundamental rights and promote a more just, equitable and inclusive society.

Most Americans would likely agree that presidents should nominate and the Senate should confirm individuals whose views on such matters can be located within the "constitutional mainstream." It is unlikely, however, that many people who endorse this view have a clear idea of how the mainstream should be defined. One working definition can be derived from a celebrated opinion written by Justice John Marshall Harlan, who was appointed to the Court by President Eisenhower in 1955. Writing about the scope of the Due Process Clause of the Fourteenth Amendment, Harlan articulated an approach to constitutional interpretation that construes fundamental liberties, not in a narrow and literal fashion, but as part of a continuum that is greater than the sum of its parts:

> The full scope of the liberty guaranteed by the Due Process Clause cannot be found in or limited by the precise terms of the specific guarantees elsewhere provided in the Constitution. This 'liberty' is not a series of isolated points pricked out in terms of the taking of property; the freedom of speech, press, and religion; the right to keep and bear arms; the freedom from unreasonable searches and seizures; and so on. It is a rational continuum which, broadly speaking, includes a freedom from all substantial arbitrary impositions and purposeless restraints . . . and which also recognizes, what a reasonable and sensitive judgment must, that certain interests require particularly careful scrutiny of the state needs asserted to justify their abridgment.

That statement has become the touchstone for a long line of substantive due process cases in which the Supreme Court has recognized a protected liberty interest under the Fourteenth Amendment in personal decisions relating to marriage, procreation, and intimate personal relationships. As the Court has affirmed, "Neither the Bill of Rights nor the specific practices of States at the time of the adoption of the Fourteenth Amendment marks the outer limits of the substantive sphere of liberty which the Fourteenth Amendment protects."

It is that approach to constitutional interpretation that remains under sharp attack from ultra-conservative judges who couch their antagonism to fundamental rights as "strict constructionism." Those claiming to be strict constructionists refuse to acknowledge constitutional rights that are not explic-

U.S. Supreme Court
Confirmation History

Of the 156 Supreme Court nominees since the court was created, 35 have been rejected or withdrawn, according to the Congressional Research Service. Most of the 35 were clustered in times of turmoil like the Civil War and Reconstruction, when politics often trumped qualifications.

In 1869, more than a century before bloggers and cable pundits would turn up the heat on nominees, President Ulysses S. Grant nominated Ebenezer Rockwood Hoar, widely considered one of the nation's top legal minds. After seven bitter weeks, the Senate voted him down, 33 to 24, in part because he had pressed for the selection of federal judges on the basis of legal talent rather than political allegiance.

Scott Shane,
"Ideology Serves as a Wild Card in Senate Debate on Court Pick,"
New York Times, *November 4, 2005.*

itly stated within the language of the Constitution itself. Thus, Justice Scalia has written in regard to reproductive choice:

> The issue is whether it is a liberty protected by the Constitution of the United States. I am sure it is not. I reach that conclusion . . . because of two simple facts: (1) the Constitution says absolutely nothing about it, and (2) the longstanding traditions of American society have permitted it to be legally proscribed.

While such restrictive theories of constitutional interpretation are favored in extreme right-wing circles, it is for the Senate to determine whether they fall within the "mainstream" or not. Before confirming nominees who share such views, senators should consider the implications for many "liberty interests" that today are taken for granted. For example, Justice Scalia's reasoning would have left in place state laws barring interracial marriage that were held unconstitutional in 1967.

As indicated above, similar doctrinal divisions can be found on such fundamental questions as the power of Congress to enact legislation under the Commerce Clause and section 5 of the Fourteenth Amendment. Such questions serve to illustrate that judicial ideology is neither an abstraction nor an irrelevancy: it lies at the core of the judicial function.

Presidents have always understood this, and have examined with care the ideology of their prospective nominees. The Senate must do so with equal diligence to ensure that judicial nominees bring to the bench not only sterling professional qualifications but also a judicial philosophy that is protective of fundamental rights and the legislation needed to effectuate them. . . .

The Proper Role of Ideology in the Confirmation Process

It is not only appropriate but necessary for both the president and the Senate to consider the myriad factors that may affect a nominee's discharge of her duties. It is proper for them to consider whether she has a genuinely open mind and whether her views will add an important perspective to the bench. It is proper for them to inquire into her beliefs about the Constitution and the role of the courts in interpreting it; her substantive views on the law and leading cases; and the philosophical ideas and attitudes that inform her view of the world. And it is proper for them to consider whether those views are sufficiently within the mainstream of legal and constitutional thought to enable her to uphold the rule of law and faithfully defend the Constitution as her oath of office requires.

It is also appropriate for the president and the Senate to consider the effect of a prospective appointment on the overall composition of the court on which the vacancy is to be filled to determine whether the nomination will preserve or enhance the ideological breadth of the court. Such considerations have particular salience when—as in the present period—ideological considerations have resulted in a conspicuous lack of balance and diversity of viewpoint in the federal courts.

It is partly for this reason that Senator Charles E. Schumer has argued that the role of ideology in the selection process should be frankly acknowledged and given "more open and rational consideration" in the course of Senate review of judicial nominees. Schumer suggests that the failure to do this has degraded the confirmation process by causing those who oppose a nominee on ideological grounds "to seek out non-ideological disqualifying factors, like small financial improprieties from long ago, to justify their opposition."

Taking ideology into account does not require senators to seek pre-commitments or "litmus tests" as to how the candidate would resolve a given case or reach a particular result, nor should they do so. Similarly, nominees should not be asked to predict how they might rule on an issue in the abstract without knowing the facts and circumstances in which it might arise. Provided that they are careful to avoid such excesses the members of the Senate are not only entitled to consider ideology as the president has done, they have a responsibility to do so. The judicial nomination and confirmation process has been described as "a means by which the people influence the development of constitutional law through their choice of presidents and senators." That can take place only if the Senate is a full partner in the process.

> *"The Senate's task of advice and consent is to advise and to query on the judicious character of nominees, not to challenge by naked power the people's will in electing who shall nominate."*

Political Ideology Is Not Relevant for Judicial Nominees

Orrin Hatch

Orrin Hatch, a Republican from Utah, was elected to the U.S. Senate in 1977 and is a member of the U.S. Senate Committee on the Judiciary. In the following viewpoint, Hatch asserts it is not the Senate committee's role to inject politics into the Senate's "advise and consent" role during judicial confirmation hearings. Once the people elect a president, Hatch asserts, that person should have the latitude to make his or her own selections with little interference from the Senate.

As you read, consider the following questions:

1. What did the author say he told Charles Schumer regarding the judicial confirmation process?

Orrin Hatch, "Statement of Orrin Hatch, United States Senator, Utah," in U.S. Senate Committee on the Judiciary, September 24, 2002.

2. How should the Senate act when there is a clear imbalance between Republicans and Democrats in the judiciary, according to the author?

3. What does the author perceive the role of the Senate to be?

Since the Democrats took over the Senate and the Judiciary Committee last June [2002] my colleague and good friend from New York [chairman of the committee, Senator Charles Schumer] has been arguing that we on the Committee should be upfront about our role in the advice and consent process—that we should not engage in the sleight-of-hand of talking about one issue while voting on another. I agree with him to the extent that we should speak and act forthrightly, and we should not stoop down to the politics of personal destruction in order to justify a vote that is based on something else.

Unfortunately, I think that is where our agreement ends. Several weeks ago on the floor, I had my friend as a captive audience because he was serving as the presiding officer, and I explained my view that being honest and open neither requires, nor excuses, the overt injection of raw politics into the advice and consent process I explained then my opinion, based on 26 years of experience, that the only way to make sense of this process is to begin with the assumption that the president's constitutional power to nominate should be given a fair amount of deference, and that we should defeat nominees only where problems are truly significant.

I believe that to the extent ideology is a question in judicial confirmations, it is a question answered by the American people and the Constitution when the president is constitutionally elected. The Senate's task of advice and consent is to advise and to query on the judicious character of nominees, not to challenge by our naked power the people's will in electing who shall nominate.

The premise of this hearing reminds me of a nickname that some clever college freshman gave to one of his required first-year courses: Introduction to the Obvious. If the point of this hearing is to show that the D.C. Circuit currently includes four judges appointed by Democrats and four appointed by Republicans, then we hardly need to convene a Senate sub-committee to figure that out. And, if the further point is made that adding one Republican appointee will result in five Republican appointees and four Democrat appointees, then I still can't imagine the hearing being disrupted by reporters running from the room yelling STOP THE PRESSES.

The Senate Must Let the President Appoint Judges

But I know that we are not here to explore the obvious with a sense of discovery. So I suppose the real question is: What should we do about this? How should the Senate act when faced with courts that have either a balance or an imbalance between the number of Republican and Democrat appointees? Should we refuse to confirm any new judges to those courts unless they belong to the right political party? Should we wait until one of the judges steps down, and then wait even longer for there to be a president who happens to belong to the same political party as the president who appointed that judge? Well, these options seem to be perfectly ludicrous to me.

The only possible answer is to accept the reality that presidents have the power to appoint judges, and that the balance in the judiciary will change over time as presidents change, but much more slowly. The variables of presidential elections, judicial retirements, circuit size, and many other factors will mean that perfect balance will be achieved rarely if ever. That is simply how the system works—and has worked, since the Judiciary Act of 1789. Our role of advice and consent is meaningful, and we must take it very seriously, but it was never intended as the power to second-guess the president or simply to substitute our judgment for his, and in doing so usurping the will of the American people.

Mr. Chairman, you know better than anyone that I am sincere about this, and that my track record proves it. Your report issued last Friday [September 20, 2002] to the press shows that I voted against only one nominee in the last ten years. As a matter of fact, you could go back a lot further than that, because that's the only one for at least the last 22 years. And to clarify, I did so not on the basis of politics or ideology, but rather out of respect for the traditional role of home-state senators in the selection of District Court nominees. When both home-state senators of that nominee informed me that they were voting no, I felt I had no choice but to respect their judgment. For what it's worth, I think that vote was quite an unfortunate episode, but I nevertheless feel that I acted in accordance with Senate practice.

In keeping with the spirit of openness and honesty, I must say this: although I know how this hearing is being billed, I am left to wonder why we are not having a hearing about the scandalous 9th Circuit, or about the procedural scandals that are plaguing the 6th Circuit. Why, I ask myself, are we having a hearing about the DC Circuit just two days before the nomination of Miguel Estrada [a judge nominated by President George W. Bush to serve on the U.S. Court of Appeals for the D.C. Circuit]. Coincidence? Surely not.

Hearings Are an Excuse To Attack Nominees

When I was chairman I ended the practice of having witnesses lined up to eviscerate good nominees. It was clear that the times had changed and that the base art native to the Potomac of destroying reputations had been too well perfected. I am glad that Chairman [Patrick] Leahy has concurred in this practice. I am disappointed that we are having this hearing because, to be frank, it strikes me that we are regressing, that

The Role of Political Ideology

[There are some who] believe that the political ideology of a candidate should be expressly considered by members of the Senate. I think that this effort is misguided and runs the risk of replacing our government of laws with one that is increasingly subject to the personal preferences of judges.

Statement by Strom Thurmond,
U.S. Senate Judiciary Committee, September 24, 2002.

this subcommittee is a just thinly veiled attempt to lay the foundation to oppose one of the most intelligent, accomplished and respected lawyers ever named to the D.C. Circuit Court. It seems to me that it would have been more forthright to name this hearing what it is: the Contra Estrada Hearing.

Now let me express my very real concern for the build up that I see happening to attempt to harm the nomination of a brilliant young man who came to this country at age 17 from another country knowing very little English and who has made his parents proud.

In one sense, I agree that there should be concern for balance on the D.C. Circuit. As chairman and founder 12 years ago of the nonpartisan Republican Hispanic Task Force—which, despite the name, is made up of both Republican and Democratic members—I have long been concerned for the inclusion of Hispanics in the federal government. Without trumpeting the overused word "diversity," I have made it my business to support the nominations of talented Hispanics for my entire career in the Senate. I am sorry that not even the desire for diversity will trump the reckless pursuit of ideology in judicial confirmations.

I have a special affinity for Hispanics and for the potential of the Latin culture in influencing the future of this country. Polls show that Latinos are the hardest working Americans, that they have strong family values and a real attachment to their faith traditions. In short, they have reinvigorated the American dream and I expect that they will bring new understandings of our nationhood that some of us might not see with tired eyes.

I also know that Hispanics come in many colors and that they have left behind countries filled with ideologues that would chain them to particular political parties. I know that they share a common sense appreciation of each other's achievements in this country without any regard whatsoever to ideology, over which some Americans have the luxury of obsessing.

Balance Is Important, But So Is Talent

I am concerned with balance on the D.C. Circuit, but of a real sort, not the kind to be discussed here today. Like President Bush, I think it is high time that a talented lawyer of Hispanic descent is represented on the second most prestigious court in the land. The D.C. Circuit hears federal cases no other court hears, and has a special role in the enforcement of the Voting Rights Act of 1965. Yes, I think that it's time that a Hispanic sat on that court.

I also think it is time that we unmask the way that Miguel Estrada's nomination is being treated, and the lengths that his detractors are going to place hurdles in its path. For months I have been sounding the alarm of the influence of the special interest groups on this committee. I have been increasingly ashamed of the axis of profits that demands that judicial nominees be voted down for a palimpsest of reasons. While the game plan is unvaried, the quarterbacks change, and now it is the liberal Hispanic groups that are on the field. They ought to be ashamed of themselves. They have sold out the aspirations of their people just to sit around schmoozing with the power elite.

I have repeatedly warned against what is going on behind the scenes. But I have done it so often that perhaps it is time to try it with new words. Well here is a Spanish word:

The word is confabular. It means: when one or more persons come together secretly to invent falsehoods about another. I am afraid that is what we will see this week against Miguel Estrada, and I am sorry, Mr. Chairman, that this hearing is part of the effort.

> *"It would be an abhorrent religious test to bar a Roman Catholic, or a Protestant, or a Jew, or an atheist, from being seated on the Court by virtue of their religious affiliation or lack thereof. But how can we not question their 'deeply held views'?"*

Religious Views Are a Relevant Consideration for U.S. Supreme Court Nominees

Annie Laurie Gaylor

Annie Laurie Gaylor is the co-president of the Freedom From Religion Foundation (FFRF). In the following essay, Gaylor maintains that although it may seem ill-advised to apply a religious litmus test to the U.S. Supreme Court confirmation process, it is essential if a nominee's deeply held religious views will influence his or her vote on important cases that will come before the Supreme Court, such as the right to an abortion, separation of church and state, and same-sex unions.

As you read, consider the following questions:

1. What did Joe Cella say about the Senate's questioning of U.S. Supreme Court nominee John Roberts's Roman Catholic convictions?

2. How can the Roman Catholic Church influence the decisions of a devout follower such as John Roberts, according to the author?

3. What does the author believe the American people have a right to know about Roberts's religious ideology?

Boosters of Supreme Court nominee John Roberts went on an immediate offense to discourage an examination of his personal Roman Catholic convictions and how they might affect his Supreme Court votes.

"A person's religious faith, and how they live that faith as an individual, has no bearing and no place in the confirmation hearing," piously intoned Joe Cella, president of Fidelis, a Catholic organization that promotes ultraconservative judges and politicians. (What would Fidelis say about an unbelieving nominee?)

Fidelis ignores the fact that it is the Roman Catholic Church that has made itself an issue, by intermeddling in American politics and the voting records of U.S. Catholic politicians.

Can Religion Influence Supreme Court Justices?

Can a truly "devout" Roman Catholic Supreme Court justice vote to uphold *Roe v. Wade* and still be in good standing, be able to take communion, and not be "gravely immoral"? Not according to the Roman Catholic Church.

The Vatican laid down the law against pro-choice Catholic public officials in its 2003 doctrinal note on participation of Catholics in political life.

> # From John F. Kennedy's 1960 Address on Religion
>
> I believe in an America that is officially neither Catholic, Protestant, nor Jewish; where no public official either requests or accept instructions on public policy from the Pope, the National Council of Churches, or any other ecclesiastical source; where no religious body seeks to impose its will directly or indirectly upon the general populace or the public acts of its officials, and where religious liberty is so indivisible that an act against one church is treated as an act against all.
>
> *John F. Kennedy, September 12, 1960.*

No less than 183 U.S. Roman Catholic bishops issued an election-year statement that politicians who support legal abortion are "cooperating in evil."

The Vatican unilaterally has warned Catholic public officials worldwide to vote in lockstep against abortion rights, gay unions and euthanasia. Such officials who do not toe the line are "not fit" to receive communion, the Vatican warned last year.

Fundamentalist Protestants as well as conservative Catholics are advancing the novel notion that it would be a "religious test for public office" to even question Roberts about his "deeply held views," as the Catholic League's Bill Donohue put it.

Religious Views Are Fair Game

Yes, it would be an abhorrent religious test to bar a Roman Catholic, or a Protestant, or a Jew, or an atheist, from being seated on the Court by virtue of their religious affiliation or lack thereof. But how can we not question their "deeply held views"?

Is it imposing a "religious test" to ask a Supreme Court nominee questions about briefs he wrote urging the overturning of *Roe vs. Wade*, defending the violent obstructionism of Operation Rescue [a Christian activist organization dedicated to ending abortion rights in the United States] as "free speech," and writing that public school students who don't want to be prayed at by clergymen at their graduation should just stay home?

American citizens have a right to know whether Roberts's devotion to his church doctrine trumps his devotion to secular rights. We need to know whether Roberts's allegiance is to the First Amendment or the First Commandment, to the Bill of Rights or right-wing papal bulls, to the Constitution or the Church, to *Roe v. Wade* or Humanae Vitae [a letter written by Pope Paul the VI in 1968 reaffirming the Catholic Church's position on abortion and contraception]. Many Catholic politicians, from JFK [President John F. Kennedy] to [2004 Democratic presidential nominee] John Kerry, have gladly volunteered answers to such questions. Why is it taboo to ask the same of Roberts?

Fundamentalists Are Getting More Aggressive

Fundamentalists who have suddenly discovered the Constitution's prohibition of a religious test for public office are meanwhile busy organizing their own religious test for Congress, the second "Justice Sunday" simulcast. The Aug. 14 [2005] event, to be broadcast via satellite to churches and Christian stations nationwide, is billed outright as a "preemptive strike" to warn Democrats not to question the Supreme Court nominee on abortion and other issues dear to the hearts of theocrats. "The Senate must bury its collective head in the sand when confronted with religious rightwing judicial nominees" is not a clause found anywhere in the U.S. Constitution.

This is sheer religious intimidation of Congress, as is the absurd attempt to paint Democrats (the traditional party of Roman Catholics) as "anti-Catholic bigots" if they dare ask pertinent questions of a Catholic nominee. Catholics, at a quarter of the U.S. population, already make up one-third of the Supreme Court and 29% of Congress, hardly an indication that "anti-Catholic bigotry" is abroad in the land.

The Senate has the right to probe whether Roberts is closer in his views to Catholic brethren Justice [Anthony] Kennedy (who, while ambivalent, has opposed an outright abortion ban), or to Justices [Antonin] Scalia and [Clarence] Thomas, who can't wait to gut the constitutional right to privacy. With abortion rights precariously hanging in the balance of this and future Supreme Court nominations, Roberts's "deeply held view" on abortion obviously is THE pivotal confirmation issue.

What Are John Roberts's Views?

Judge Roberts, have you, or have you not, ever been a supporter of the separation of church and state?

It is not reassuring that Christian Coalition president Roberta Combs, perhaps with pun intended, promised that Roberts "would faithfully interpret the Constitution." Not surprisingly, Troy Newman, president of Operation Rescue, the Christian antiabortion group Roberts defended on behalf of the government, exalted: "We pray that Roberts will be swiftly confirmed." What do they know that we don't? And why should we not know it, too?

As Sen. [Patrick] Leahy put it: "No one is entitled to a free pass to a lifetime appointment to the Supreme Court."

The right-wing religious lobby is bent on curtailing questioning before the hearings have even begun. This alarming intent by right-wing religionists to continue to muzzle open debate over judicial nominees should not be countenanced.

> *"There is a clear provision in the United States Constitution, Article VI Clause 3, which provides that there shall be no religious tests for federal office."*

There Should Not Be a Religious Litmus Test for U.S. Supreme Court Nominees

Stephen B. Presser and Charles E. Rice

Stephen B. Presser is a professor at Northwestern University School of Law in Chicago and legal affairs editor for Chronicles, *a conservative journal. Charles E. Rice is professor emeritus at Notre Dame Law School. In the following viewpoint, Presser and Rice are dismayed by the prospect that John Roberts's devout Catholicism would deter some senators from voting for his confirmation when he is obviously, in their view, a well-qualified U.S. Supreme Court nominee. They argue that although a nominee's religion can be taken into account, it cannot be used to automatically disqualify him or her.*

As you read, consider the following questions:

1. What do the authors cite as John Roberts's qualifications to the U.S. Supreme Court?

Stephen B. Presser and Charles E. Rice, "Religious Tests," *National Review*, September 13, 2005. Copyright © 2005 National Review, Inc., 215 Lexington Avenue, New York, NY 10016. Reproduced by permission.

2. According to the authors, why wouldn't a devout, practicing Catholic be confirmed, in the view of some senators?

3. What are some recent examples of senators questioning a political nominee's religion?

In recent memory there have rarely been nominees to the Supreme Court with credentials as distinguished as John Roberts.

He is a graduate of Harvard College and Harvard Law School; he had clerkships with two judges, [U.S. Court of Appeals Judge Henry J.] Friendly and [Justice William] Rehnquist, spoken of in hushed tones by those who care about those sorts of things; he amassed a record as a brilliant advocate before the United States Supreme Court (to whose arguments Supreme Court clerks—a jaded group—would come for edification).

With a record like that, Roberts could be expected to sail through his confirmation hearings and become the next chief justice of the Supreme Court.

Roberts's Confirmation Challenge

There are rumblings, though, that Roberts's religion—he's Catholic—could be raised against him, and there are dark intimations coming from some quarters of the Senate and some liberal advocacy groups that a practicing Catholic who takes church teachings seriously cannot be trusted to assume a position on the Court.

The idea seems to be that since the Church is firmly opposed to abortion, the death penalty, and homosexual marriage, Roberts could not, consistently with his deeply held religious beliefs, even-handedly administer justice in these areas.

Perhaps it is a mark of the desperation of Roberts's opponents that his religion is now being raised against him, but those of us who believe in the Constitution and in the objec-

---

Religion and the U.S. Supreme Court

Any nominee to the Supreme Court worth his or her salt will testify before the Senate Judiciary Committee that personal religious belief is completely irrelevant to his or her work as a Supreme Court justice. Logically speaking, one's private beliefs about theology really have no bearing on one's interpretive methodology of the Constitution. Everyone agrees to this proposition, but it is a formal one, and it does not deal with the psychological reality of religion as a parallel internal belief system that figures highly in the justice's overall intellectual and moral makeup.

The real question is whether a justice's philosophical approach to religion reflects or mirrors his or her philosophical approach to law, which is what we mean by jurisprudence. To a certain extent, it almost inescapably and inevitably does. The justices who have an authoritarian approach to religion and spiritual life tend to read the Constitution and law as rigidly establishing the structures of governmental power over citizens.

Conversely, justices who tend to side privately, as far as I can tell, with more liberal religious currents and to favor tolerance over dogma also try to read the Constitution as a charter of individual rights and to interpret its structural provisions through the lens of freedom and individual dignity.

Jamie Raskin, "Religion & the Supreme Court,"
Moment, *September–October 2008.*

---

tive interpretation of that document need to cut off the head of this argument and drive a stake through its heart before it does further damage.

Religious Discrimination Is Anti-American

There is a clear provision in the United States Constitution, Article VI Clause 3, which provides that there shall be no religious tests for federal office. This reflects the belief of the framers that one's religion is a matter between one's God and one's self, and should not play a role in determining suitability for public office.

The notion that Catholics, Protestants, Jews, or adherents of any other religion need not apply is utterly foreign to our Constitutional traditions, however much religious bigotry was an evil undercurrent in our popular history.

Senate hearings over Supreme Court nominees are a fairly new phenomenon, and until the fourth decade of the 20th century it was rare for nominees even to appear in person at hearings over their nomination. Historically, there have been nominations to the court—Justice [Louis] Brandeis comes to mind—where religion was whispered about as a disqualifying factor.

Recent Confirmation Debacles

In more recent history, nominations to the Court have become political circuses, or perhaps ideological wars, even to the point of the nominee's religion being called into question.

During the confirmation hearings of former Attorney General John Ashcroft, Senate Minority Leader Harry Reid said "I think we have a right to look into John Ashcroft's religion." During Judge William Pryor's confirmation hearings for a federal bench in Atlanta, Senator Charles Schumer said he was troubled by his "deeply held personal beliefs."

Such incivility has even extended beyond confirmation hearings. Just this past June, Senator Tom Harkin said this of Christian broadcasters: "They are sort of our own home grown Taliban."

The upcoming hearings and floor debate should be devoid of such remarks.

There Must Be a Line

It is legitimate for the Senate to explore with Judge Roberts his philosophy of judging, and perhaps even his beliefs about the connection between law and morality. It is indisputably true that our earliest federal judges believed that we could have no order without law, no law without morality, and no morality without religion. These may be general matters about which Judge Roberts could be enlightening to his Senate questioners.

For them, or for anyone else to suggest, however, that the fact that he adheres to any particular religion is a disqualification for office would be to embrace, at least analogously, the evil sought to be prevented by the Constitutional prohibition of religious tests. It would also reveal an intolerance of a kind that has no place in the Senate or any other part of American life.

While most senators will likely be sensitive to the issue of religious faith, we are rightly concerned especially about activist groups which have staked their reputations on Roberts's defeat.

Roberts Is a Fine Nominee

Everything we know about Judge Roberts at this point suggests that he is that very rare breed of American lawyer who believes that the duty of a judge is objectively and fairly to apply the law whatever his personal or religious predilections.

His religion ought to be off-limits in his confirmation hearings, as it should be for any nominee.

"Judicial independence is important, but so is judicial accountability. Appointing Supreme Court justices to fixed terms would balance the two competing principles."

There Should Be Term Limits for U.S. Supreme Court Justices

Doug Bandow

Doug Bandow is the vice president of policy for Citizen Outreach, a public policy group dedicated to limiting or reducing the powers of governments, and a fellow at the American Conservative Defense Alliance, a Washington, D.C., group that advances conservative national security and foreign policies. In the following viewpoint, Bandow explores the negative consequences of lifetime tenure for U.S. Supreme Court justices, such as a tendency to settle into comfortable patterns of thinking and increasing judicial activism. Bandow recommends appointing justices not to life terms but to fixed terms of 10–12 years, which he feels would provide an element of judicial accountability.

Doug Bandow, "A Way to End Bitter Fights over Justices," *Los Angeles Times*, March 2, 2005. Copyright © 2005 *Los Angeles Times*. Reproduced by permission of the author.

As you read, consider the following questions:

1. Before 1970, what was the average term served by a U.S. Supreme Court justice?

2. What has been the average term of a Supreme Court justice since 1970?

3. What advantages does Bandow cite for appointing justices to fixed terms?

An activist judiciary has joined the legislative and executive branches in making public policy. The influence of judges has been magnified by their relative immunity from political pressure. Although the courts sometimes follow the election returns, in many cases, such as abortion, judicial decisions have short-circuited normal political discourse.

The Downside of Life Tenure

That fact alone makes judicial appointments important. Their significance is increased by life tenure enjoyed by federal judges, particularly Supreme Court justices. Lose the battle over filling a Supreme Court slot and you suffer the consequences for decades.

There are other consequences of lifetime tenure. The appointment process has become ever more arbitrary as judges hang on despite advancing age.

The last justice to retire [as of 2005] was William Blackmun in 1994. He served 24 years. Before 1970, the average term served was a bit over 15 years. Since 1970, justices have averaged 25.5 years. The age at retirement has jumped a decade, to nearly 79. Today, only Clarence Thomas is under the traditional retirement age of 65.

Most Supreme Court members have avoided obvious infirmity. However, William O. Douglas, who served more than 36 years before retiring in 1975, was evidently failing after a stroke. Chief Justice William Howard Taft pressured ailing As-

Abuses of Lifetime Tenure

The current system of life tenure leads to many abuses. Justices time their departures strategically to give presidents they like an appointment. Presidents appoint young candidates to the Court in place of 60-year-olds to maximize their impact on the Court. We believe that Senate confirmations are more bitter because all involved know that they are picking someone who may end up serving 35 years instead of 18, making the stakes much higher.

Steven G. Calabresi and James Lindgren,
"Justice for Life?" Wall Street Journal, April 10, 2005.

sociate Justice Joseph McKenna to quit in 1925. Current Chief Justice William Rehnquist is seriously ill with thyroid cancer.

Another concern is that long-serving justices tend to be less conversant with current culture. Proper constitutional interpretation obviously can survive a lack of familiarity with, say, rap music. More serious, however, is the concern that comfortable patterns of thinking can go unchallenged for years.

Positive Aspects of Lifetime Tenure

The justification for life tenure is most obviously history: It is enshrined in the Constitution. More important, lifetime appointments help insulate the courts from transient political pressures.

Such protection is necessary if judges are to sometimes make unpopular decisions upholding the nation's fundamental law. And judicial independence is important. Critics of judicial overreaching have proposed a number of steps—limiting court jurisdiction or impeaching errant jurists, for instance—that could be abused.

Still, the judiciary, no less than the executive and legislative branches, must be held accountable. Unreviewable power is always dangerous.

Implement Term Limits

The best means of responding to these concerns is to appoint judges to fixed terms rather than for life. Ten or 12 years would allow extended service while ensuring turnover.

The advantages of such a step would be many. First, judicial nominations no longer would become political Armageddon. Supreme Court appointments would always be important, but there would be less incentive to vilify and filibuster nominees. After all, the new justice would serve only one term. Moreover, term limits would ensure a steady transformation of the court's membership. An enfeebled justice could not hang on in an attempt to outlast a president. New members at regular intervals would encourage intellectual as well as physical rejuvenation of the court.

Most important, fixed terms would improve judicial accountability. Judges still would be independent, largely insulated from attack. However, elective officials could eventually reassert control without doing violence to the judicial institution. Yet it still would not be easy, and the process would allow time for ephemeral popular passions to subside.

Judicial independence is important, but so is judicial accountability. Appointing Supreme Court justices to fixed terms would balance the two competing principles.

> "[Public opinion] makes the Supreme Court a little more democratic—and a little less like a real court, the judges of which are proudly indifferent to public opinion."

There Are Advantages and Disadvantages to Term Limits for U.S. Supreme Court Justices

Richard A. Posner

Richard A. Posner is a judge on the U.S. Court of Appeals for the Seventh Circuit Court, a lecturer at the University of Chicago Law School, and a prolific author on such subjects as jurisprudence and legal philosophy. In the following viewpoint, Posner finds the arguments in favor of term limits unconvincing, proposing solutions for problems brought on by lifetime tenure. He also delineates several problems with applying fixed term limits for U.S. Supreme Court justices.

As you read, consider the following questions:

1. What does the author list as serious drawbacks to term limits for judges?

2. According to the author, how would offering senior status address the problem of judges shirking their duties?

3. Does the author believe diminished mental acuity caused by aging is a good argument for term limits?

Whether in the academy or in the judiciary, life tenure guarantees independence but also invites abuse because it eliminates any penalty for shirking. More precisely, it reduces the penalty, because if salary can vary, the employer can penalize the tenured employee by denying him raises, though reducing his salary would presumably violate the terms of the tenure contract. The federal judicial salary structure makes dealing with shirkers impossible. Judges do not receive merit raises; when the judicial wage is raised, it is raised for all. Rightly so—performance-based criteria for judicial compensation would compromise judicial independence because of the absence of objective performance measures.

Fixed but Renewable Terms

So would a fixed but renewable term. Granted, this is the approach that has been taken, with no untoward results as far as I know, with respect to federal magistrate judges and bankruptcy judges. They are appointed for 8-year and 14-year renewable terms, respectively. But ..., they are appointed by judges rather than by political officials. In any event, a *nonre*newable fixed term would not compromise judicial independence. A term of, say, 10 years would limit the length of service of the shirkers and also create an incentive for good performance because the judge would want to secure a good job after his judicial term expired. But there are serious drawbacks, illuminated by the literature on term limits for legislators. Judges would be distracted by having to make arrangements for another job at the expiration of their terms; their decisions might be distorted by the desire to curry favor with potential future employers; and more rapid turnover of judges would reduce legal stability. The first two tendencies illustrate what economists call the "last period" problem. When a worker knows that he is soon to retire or quit, his commitment to his job may dwindle. Yet none of these concerns might be decisive were it not that candidates for federal judgeships are carefully screened, which eliminates from the appointment pool the candidates most likely to shirk. An additional effect of fixed terms would be to increase the president's power to change the political composition of the federal judiciary; . . . judges tend to time retirement in such a way that their successors are of the same party.

Senior Status

Senior status is an ingenious carrot-stick response to the problem of shirking. It allows judges, after they become eligible to retire, to continue working, at no reduction in pay, provided they are willing to shoulder at least one-third of an active judge's workload. This is an attractive offer, and most eligible judges accept it when, or within a few years after, they become eligible. But part of the deal is that a senior judge can be barred (though with no diminution in pay) from judging by the chief judge of his court subject to review by the court's judicial council. Senior status is thus a variant of the buyout schemes by which universities and other employers forbidden by law to fix a mandatory retirement age try to induce retirement.

The case for term limits for Supreme Court justices is stronger than that for judges of the lower federal courts. If I am right that it is a political court, the absence of term limits is an affront to democratic theory; conferring life tenure on politicians is profoundly undemocratic. Moreover, the Justices

Alexander Hamilton and Term Limits

That inflexible and uniform adherence to the rights of the Constitution, and of individuals, which we perceive to be indispensable in the courts of justice, can certainly not be expected from judges who hold their offices by a temporary commission. Periodical appointments, however regulated, or by whomsoever made, would, in some way or other, be fatal to their necessary independence. If the power of making them was committed either to the executive or legislature, there would be danger of an improper complaisance to the branch which possessed it; if to both, there would be an unwillingness to hazard the displeasure of either; if to the people, or to persons chosen by them for the special purpose, there would be too great a disposition to consult popularity, to justify a reliance that nothing would be consulted but the Constitution and the laws.

Alexander Hamilton, The Federalist No. 78:
The Judiciary Department, June 14, 1788.

are ineligible for senior status; that is, they cannot sit part-time on the Supreme Court after retiring, though they can if they want to sit in the lower federal courts. So they do not have the same incentive that lower-court judges do to semiretire. With increasing longevity, justices are likely to be serving very long terms into very old age.

What Other Countries Do

We can gain insight into the tenure issue from the literature on constitutional courts in other countries. [Constitutional scholars John] Ferejohn and [Pasquale] Pasquino argue that the limited, nonrenewable terms (usually 10 or 12 years) of the judges of these courts are one reason such courts are less controversial than our Supreme Court, despite lacking the protective coloration that our Court gets from having a non-constitutional jurisdiction as well as its constitutional one and deciding "real" cases in the standard manner (opposing parties, briefs, oral argument). Shorter terms mean that judicial appointments are less consequential and therefore attract less public attention and controversy. And foreign constitutional courts usually operate without oral arguments, signed opinions, or published dissents, so there is less opportunity for the judges to play to the gallery than there is for our justices to do so. Our gallery, however, is the court of public opinion, and its participation in constitutional controversies injects a democratic element into constitutional adjudication. It makes the Supreme Court a little more democratic—and a little less like a real court, the judges of which are proudly indifferent to public opinion. Not that they should brag about that; their indifference to public opinion is the mirror of the public's indifference to them.

Mental Acuity Is Not an Issue

What is not a good argument for judicial term limits is that elderly people tend to experience diminished mental acuity. They do; but there are a few professions, such as history, theology, literary criticism and scholarship, and philosophy, in which the negative correlation between age and performance is weak. Judging is one of them, though part of the reason is that judges in our system are appointed at relatively advanced ages; this means that early decliners tend to be screened out and judges tend not to get bored, or run dry, at the same age at which persons in other fields do who have been in the same line of work for many years.

Even apart from exceptionally able judges, such as [Oliver Wendell] Holmes, [Louis] Brandeis, [Billings] Learned Hand,

and Henry Friendly, who performed with distinction well into their 80s (Holmes served into his 90s, but was fading toward the end), the federal judiciary in general exhibits little age-related decline in quality or (apart from senior status) even quantity of performance. And this is further evidence against an algorithmic model of the judicial process. Were judging highly analytical, we would expect a pronounced aging effect, as in other analytical fields, such as mathematics and physics. It is also an explanation for the legalist character of the foreign career judiciaries. A career judiciary has a lower age profile than a lateral-entry one because the lowest tier of judges consists of recent law school graduates. Young judges have good analytic skills but little experience. Older judges have the experience that younger judges lack, making them abler to play the occasional-legislator role because that role is not algorithmic but depends instead on insight into policy.

Periodical Bibliography

The following articles have been selected to supplement the diverse views presented in this chapter.

Emily Bazelon	"Answer the Question, Judge!" *Slate*, July 26, 2005. www.slate.com/id/2123413/.
Ruth Conniff	"Time for Tough Questions," *Progressive*, July 20, 2005. http://66.170.18.163/mag_rcb072005.
Gene Healy	"Bush's Tortuous Choice," Cato Institute, July 15, 2005. www.cato.org/ pub_display.php?pub_id=3991.
Karen Houppert	"Curbing Abortion Rights," *Nation*, April 18, 2007. www.thenation.com/doc/20070430/ houppert.
John P. Hubert	"The 'Fruits' of Legal Positivism: Utilitarianism in Action," *IntellectualConservative.com*, December 9, 2005.
Jeff Jacoby	"Supreme Court Term Limits," *Boston Globe*, September 7, 2005. www.boston.com/news/ globe/editorial_opinion/oped/articles/2005/09/ 07/supreme_court_term_limits.
Roger Pilon	"McCarthy Liberals," *New York Post*, July 29, 2005.
Bruce Shapiro	"Compromised and Corrupted," *Nation*, July 13, 2006. www.thenation.com/doc/20060130/ shapiro2.
David Yerushalmi	"Jurisprudence, Certainty, and the Alito Hearings," *American Spectator*, January 17, 2006. http://spectator.org/archives/2006/01/17/ jurisprudence-certainty-and-th.

What Should Be the
Judicial Philosophy of
the U.S. Supreme Court?

Chapter Preface

O ver the past few decades, the debate over the concept of "judicial activism" has been central to considerations of the U.S. judicial system, particularly the U.S. Supreme Court. Both conservative and liberal commentators have decried— and on occasion applauded—what they perceive as the judicial activism of certain justices and Court decisions. Judicial activism is a way of interpreting the Constitution that allows justices to factor in the prevailing attitudes of the era and the needs of the nation when deciding how they are going to rule on court cases. The counter to judicial activism is the idea of judicial restraint, which refers to judges deciding cases strictly on the wording and dictates of the U.S. Constitution.

In general use, "judicial activism" is a pejorative term to describe judges who go beyond their defined and perceived appropriate judicial duties and begin to influence public policies. Critics charge that practitioners of judicial activism are too eager to abandon the literal words of the Constitution and to twist the meanings of those words in favor of ideological decisions that fit the social norms of the times. These critics argue that under the Constitution, such decisions should be left to the legislative power of the states. One of the most often cited examples of judicial activism is *Roe v. Wade* (1973), the controversial Supreme Court decision that struck down restrictive abortion laws as violating the right to privacy inherent in the due process clause of the Fourteenth Amendment of the Constitution.

Defenders of judicial activism point out that the practice is essential to hold Congress and state and local governments to their constitutional boundaries and to protect individual liberties and the rule of law. In addition, they argue conservatives and liberals decry the practice of judicial activism when it suits them—usually when a decision is handed down that they oppose on ideological grounds.

Judicial activism is a charge that has been leveled by both sides of the political spectrum. Both Democrats and Republicans have accused judges of activism in recent decades. Supreme Courts under the politically varied administrations of Franklin Roosevelt, Richard Nixon, Ronald Reagan, and Bill Clinton were all accused of judicial activism.

The practice of judicial activism is discussed in viewpoints in the following chapter, which focuses on the judicial philosophy of the U.S. Supreme Court. The viewpoints presented also explore the concept of originalism and the use of foreign laws and court decisions in Supreme Court cases.

> "Stripped of its rhetoric, the hostility to-
> wards citing foreign decisions in any
> context seems misplaced."

The U.S. Supreme Court Should Refer to Foreign Court Decisions

Austen L. Parrish

*Austen L. Parrish is an associate professor of law at Southwest-
ern Law School in Los Angeles. In the following viewpoint, Parrish explores the legitimacy of the U.S. Supreme Court's use of
foreign law in deciding cases. Parrish characterizes the backlash
against this practice as misplaced and ill-considered, as well as
inconsistent with U.S. judicial history.*

As you read, consider the following questions:

1. According to the author, how have some senators re-
   acted to the use of foreign sources in U.S. Supreme
   Court decisions?

2. What are the two assertions critics make regarding the
   use of foreign law in the Supreme Court?

Austen L. Parrish, "Storm in a Teacup," *University of Illinois Law Review*, 2007, pp. 639–
642. Copyright © 2007 University of Illinois, College of Law. Reproduced by permission.

3. What effect does the author believe using foreign laws can have?

Few topics have captured the legal community's imagination and invoked such passion as the recent [2006] debate over the use of foreign law in U.S. Supreme Court decisions. The Supreme Court justices have publicly debated the topic. Congress has attempted to enact sweeping laws barring judges from using foreign sources, while some senators have suggested that citation to a foreign source should be an impeachable offense. Mere mention of foreign law in an opinion triggers vitriolic responses from Justice [Antonin] Scalia and, sometimes, Justice [Clarence] Thomas. Even circuit court judges have weighed in on the debate. Legal scholars are not above the fray. A spate of recent scholarly commentary has condemned the use of foreign law. One professor has gone so far as to belittle justices who dare cite to foreign opinions, remarkably suggesting that its use is evidence of intellectual inferiority.

Bereft of nuance, this debate has become one of stark absolutes. Those who condemn the practice of citing to foreign law argue that its use should be banned *in toto* [completely]. They variously assert that citation to foreign law undermines (1) the Court's legitimacy by impermissibly expanding judicial discretion and (2) our national and democratic sovereignty. On the other hand, despite numerous writings extolling the virtues of comparative constitutionalism, the amount of recent scholarship that strongly advocates the use of foreign sources, while also providing a theory justifying that use, is meager. Justice [Stephen] Breyer and Justice [Anthony] Kennedy—often seen as the leading proponents for citing foreign sources—respond defensively, if not with bewilderment, as to why the debate ensues. Rarely do they or other proponents affirmatively articulate why the arguments opposing the use of foreign law are unfounded on their own terms. And often the scholarship fails to explain how the use of foreign law should be commended as being consistent with American constitutionalism.

Yet it is consistent. Stripped of its rhetoric, the hostility towards citing foreign decisions in any context seems misplaced. Those who oppose the use of foreign law confuse the question of validity with the question of what weight to afford that law. The critics also ignore a history of practice in which foreign legal materials have been used in constitutional analysis. Indeed, the practice is one our state courts have long embraced when interpreting their own, unique state constitutions, a point that until now has been downplayed. Lurking under the surface of arguments made by those who oppose the use of foreign sources appears to be the hubris of American exceptionalism. More fundamentally, the arguments often reflect particular modes of constitutional interpretation—textualism and originalism—that, despite recent attempts to resuscitate, the legal mainstream long ago rejected or discounted, at least in their extreme forms. A need therefore remains to explain not only why the use of foreign law is not offensive, but why its use is consistent with American constitutionalism and the proper role of the judiciary. . . .

This is not an academic exercise: explaining why the U.S. Supreme Court's use of foreign law is legitimate, while debunking arguments that categorically reject its use is important. The spirited backlash against the judiciary for citing to foreign materials as persuasive authority threatens to have a chilling effect. Instead of exploring how to utilize foreign materials in a refined way, the debate has been debased to an all-or-nothing proposition, with extreme and fringe positions obtaining a degree of superficial credibility. The result is problematic, and its impact real. Lessons that could be learned from other countries are missed. Moreover, the Court's failure to engage more meaningfully with foreign law divorces the Court from an ongoing transnational dialogue that is develop-

History of Foreign Law in American Jurisprudence

The United States Supreme Court has made references to foreign law since the earliest days of the Republic. During the tenure of Chief Justice John Marshall, the Court was often called on to interpret treaties and weigh controversies involving ships on the high seas, and the Justices frequently cited the laws of other nations in their decisions. In 1829, for example, Marshall analyzed both Spanish and French law to settle a claim by an American who had bought a parcel of land once owned by Spain and later included in the Louisiana Purchase. Contemporary commercial disputes also cross borders, and the Justices rely on foreign and international law, as well as on American statutes, to adjudicate them. In the past two years, the Court has considered such questions as whether Mexican trucks must abide by American safety rules under NAFTA [North American Free Trade Agreement], whether the American family of a Holocaust victim could recover art seized by the Nazis in Austria, and whether a United States district court should compel the American computer-chip-makers AMD [Advanced Micro Chip] and Intel to provide documents to each other in a European antitrust dispute. "When it comes to interpreting treaties or settling international business disputes, the Court has always looked to the laws of other countries, and the practice has not been particularly controversial," says Norman Dorsen, a professor at New York University Law School.

Jeffrey Toobin, "Swing Shift,"
New Yorker, September 12, 2005.

ing and shaping international norms—norms that, one day, may exert some control domestically. . . .

The U.S. Supreme Court should continue cautiously to use foreign law as persuasive authority. Engaging in transnational constitutional dialogue is a commendable goal, not an illegitimate one.

> "It's time for the American people to let the justices, and all future judicial nominees, know that we believe it is their duty to base their decisions on the U.S. Constitution, and that it is a violation of their oath of office to base decisions on foreign decisions or practices."

The U.S. Supreme Court Should Not Refer to Foreign Court Decisions

Phyllis Schlafly

Phyllis Schlafly is a conservative commentator, columnist, author, and founder of the pro-family organization, the Eagle Forum. In the following viewpoint, Schlafly criticizes the increasing citation of foreign laws in U.S. Supreme Court decisions, arguing that some justices want to sidestep the democratic process by changing the U.S. Constitution through judicial means.

Phyllis Schlafly, "Who Is the Supreme Court Listening To?" *Eagle Forum*, November 4, 2004. Reproduced by permission of the author.

As you read, consider the following questions:

1. What did former Justice Sandra Day O'Connor say about the use of international law in Supreme Court decisions?

2. According to the author, how did international law influence the U.S. Supreme Court decision in *Lawrence v. Texas*?

3. What did Justice Antonin Scalia write about using foreign laws in Supreme Court decisions?

Globalism doesn't mean just accepting foreign countries' products and people across our borders. Supreme Court justices are beginning to manifest a curious fascination with foreign legal systems, too.

Speaking at Bill Clinton's alma mater on October 26 [2004], Justice Sandra Day O'Connor told the Georgetown audience that international law "is vital if judges are to faithfully discharge their duties." She was dedicating Georgetown's new international law center.

"International law is a help in our search for a more peaceful world," O'Connor declared in her address, omitting to mention that every attempt to use international law and leagues has been an abysmal failure in preventing war. Besides, the U.S. Constitution gives Congress, not the Supreme Court or any international body, the authority to declare war.

Insidious Motives

The effort to import international law into the United States has nothing to do with preventing war. The purpose is to change our Constitution without obtaining approval of the American people through the amendment process.

The Supreme Court recently accepted amicus [friend of the court] briefs from Mikhail Gorbachev and from 48 foreign countries in a case considered this fall involving the death penalty for juveniles, *Roper v. Simmons*. You read that right; the High Court is listening to Gorbachev's opinion about what U.S. criminal law should be!

The justices have increasingly cited foreign law to try to undo our death penalty, even though the U.S. Constitution in several places expressly recognizes its legality. However, the justices are very selective about which countries they cite, since executions are common in many countries.

Nor do the judges cite stricter abortion laws around the world as they strike down state and congressional bans on partial-birth abortion.

Foreign Laws Should Not Influence Us

Earlier this year [2004], the Supreme Court allowed the Commission of the European Communities for the first time in history to present oral argument as a friend of the Court. This foreign governmental body was not even a party in the dispute between Intel and Advanced Micro Devices, yet the justices granted it a special right to argue that is rarely conferred even on American entities.

The Supreme Court's famous sodomy ruling, *Lawrence v. Texas*, which encouraged the current push toward same-sex marriage licenses, was based on references to the European Court of Human Rights and other foreign sources as examples of "emerging awareness" about sex. But that opinion, written by Justice Anthony Kennedy, conveniently omitted any reference to countries, such as India, where homosexual behavior is a crime meriting imprisonment.

In her Georgetown speech, O'Connor bragged that "we operate today under a very large array of international agreements, treaties, organizations." Such language is reminiscent of Bill Clinton's boast to the United Nations that he was pushing the United States into a "web of institutions and arrangements" for "the emerging international system."

Using Foreign Law in Supreme Court Decisions

Right now out of the sight of most Americans is a quiet movement to allow the legal decision-making process of the U.S. Supreme Court to incorporate judicial findings of law from countries like France, Germany, the Netherlands, Aruba or even Jamaica. . . . We may want to vacation in Jamaica but I don't think we want to have our cases decided on their legal precedents, or Aruba, with their top notch legal sleuthing. . . .

The Supreme Court of our nation has a small number of justices who feel very strongly that our Constitutional Law, our American legal precedents, our American values which help to shape, help to build and construct the very foundation of American jurisprudence . . . well it's just not good enough to use to assist the three justices in coming to an American made constitutional conclusion. [Anthony] Kennedy, [Ruth Bader] Ginsberg and [Stephen] Breyer wish to look for their legal remedies outside our borders.

Kevin Fobbs,
"Using Foreign Law Is the Real Supreme Court Test,"
gopusa.com, September 10, 2005.

International agreements usually have negative fallout. One law enforcement expert dubbed NAFTA [North American Free Trade Agreement] the North American Free Trafficking Agreement because it has greatly expanded illegal drug smuggling into our country.

Heed the Oath

Section 3331 of Title 5 of the U.S. Code requires high-ranking officers, including Supreme Court justices, to take this oath:

"I, ___, do solemnly swear (or affirm) that I will support and defend the Constitution of the United States against all enemies, foreign and domestic; that I will bear true faith and allegiance to the same; that I take this obligation freely, without any mental reservation or purpose of evasion; and that I will well and faithfully discharge the duties of the office on which I am about to enter. So help me God."

Violation of this oath should be an impeachable offense.

Yet, six of the nine Supreme Court justices are now on record using references to foreign law in their opinions. In a speech last year [2003], Justice Ruth Bader Ginsburg told the American Constitution Society that "your perspective on constitutional law should encompass the world."

Three Supreme Court justices disagree. Most Americans would agree with Justice Antonin Scalia, who wrote that the Court should not "impose foreign moods, fads or fashions on Americans."

It's time for the American people to let the justices, and all future judicial nominees, know that we believe it is their duty to base their decisions on the U.S. Constitution, and that it is a violation of their oath of office to base decisions on foreign decisions or practices.

> *"Judicial activism—defined as courts holding the president, Congress, and state and local governments to their constitutional boundaries—is essential to protecting individual liberty and the rule of law."*

Judicial Activism Is Necessary in Certain Circumstances

Clint Bolick

Clint Bolick is senior fellow at the Goldwater Institute in Phoenix and a conservative author. In the following viewpoint, Bolick acknowledges the practice of judicial activism has become a pejorative amongst conservatives and liberals, but he argues if it is defined as reminding the other branches of government of their constitutional boundaries, it is vital to the rule of law. Bolick asserts judicial activism must correct legislative overreaching and protect individual rights.

As you read, consider the following questions:

1. According to the author, how did the framers of the Constitution feel about the concept of judicial review?

2. How does the author explain former Chief Justice William Rehnquist's record of judicial activism while on the U.S. Supreme Court?

3. What does the author cite as a bigger problem than judicial activism?

Judicial activism has become a universal pejorative, a rare point of agreement between red and blue America. Conservatives and liberals alike condemn courts for overturning policy decisions they support. Both sides would reduce the judiciary's constitutional scrutiny of the actions of other branches of government—a role it exercises not too much but far too little.

To be sure, courts deserve criticism when they exercise legislative or executive powers—ordering taxes to be raised, assuming control over school systems or prisons, or as the Supreme Court did yesterday [April 2, 2007], giving regulatory agencies broad lawmaking authority. But better to call this behavior what it really is, which is not "activism" but lawlessness. By contrast, judicial activism—defined as courts holding the president, Congress, and state and local governments to their constitutional boundaries—is essential to protecting individual liberty and the rule of law.

The Positive Side of Judicial Activism

Judicial review, the power to invalidate unconstitutional laws, was essential to the scheme of republican government established by our Constitution. The courts, declared James Madison, would provide "an impenetrable bulwark against every assumption of power in the executive and legislative" branches, and "will naturally be led to resist every encroachment of rights expressly stipulated for in the Constitution by the declaration of rights."

Conservatives have long attacked judicial activism; more recently liberals have joined the chorus. Now that the welfare state and other cherished policy objectives are enshrined in law, many liberals heed Justice Stephen Breyer's call for "judicial modesty." The liberals' newfound self-restraint permeated the Supreme Court confirmation hearings of John Roberts and Samuel Alito, who were accused of predilections toward conservative judicial activism.

Liberal critics cite statistics showing that the Supreme Court under Chief Justice William Rehnquist was more activist in invalidating federal laws than any of its predecessors. True. But the number of decisions striking down executive and legislative actions pales in comparison to the growth of federal laws and regulations during the same period. It took 169 years from the founding for the federal code of laws to reach 11,472 pages—and only four decades more for that number to quadruple. In 1960, the Code of Federal Regulations numbered 22,000 pages; today that number has grown by more than 700%.

Deference Is Overrated

Advocates of judicial deference contend that courts are ill-equipped to second-guess legislative determinations. If legislators carefully pondered the merits and constitutionality of legislation, that argument might have merit. But our legislators rarely even read the complex bills they pass, which all too often are manipulated by outside interests. Judges, by contrast, carefully sift through competing evidence presented by both sides. And they should. Courts that merely rubber-stamp legislation or executive branch decisions out of bland, or blind, "deference" evade their essential constitutional role.

Moreover, judicial deference to "democratic processes" is beside the point, given the proliferation of laws and regulations created by bureaucrats who are not in *any* meaningful way democratically accountable. And not only at the federal level.

What Is Judicial Activism?

The first step is to clarify the debate. Striking down an unconstitutional law, even one supported by a popular majority, is not judicial activism. Assuming the powers of other branches or arriving at decisions with no basis in the Constitution, as understood by those who ratified it, is activism even when the ruling accomplishes a noble result.

W. James Antle, "Who Are You Calling Activist?"
American Spectator, *August 4, 2005.*

The most explosive growth in local governments in recent decades has occurred in special districts and regional authorities that typically are accountable (if at all) to politicians, not voters. Ironically, courts typically defer to the "expertise" of regulatory bodies, rather than carefully scrutinizing their actions for compliance, not only with constitutional commands, but even to the vast legislative and executive powers that have been delegated to them.

Attacks on Judicial Activism Are Weak

At bottom, liberal and conservative attacks on judicial activism are hopelessly subjective and inconsistent. Take two cases from the 1990s. In one, the U.S. Supreme Court struck down a Colorado law that forbade local governments from enacting antidiscrimination laws that protected homosexuals. In another, the Court struck down a New Jersey law that forbade the Boy Scouts from excluding homosexuals. In both cases, the Court protected freedom of association, finding an exercise of democratic power at the state level unconstitutional. Similar cases, similar principles, identical results.

Most liberals supported the result in the first case, condemning the second as judicial activism; most conservatives did precisely the opposite. What critics on both left and right really object to is the neutral application of constitutional principles when it hampers their own desired policy outcomes.

The Real Threat Comes from Another Direction

While judicial activism is the subject of spirited attack, the far greater problem is judicial abdication of its core constitutional duty to protect individual rights. Courts routinely apply a presumption of constitutionality to most governmental enactments that skews the playing field against individuals whose rights are violated. Far worse, courts have read out of the Constitution vitally important protections of individual rights, such as the constraints against government interference with the sanctity of contract and the privileges or immunities of citizenship.

As the framers understood, these are not esoteric issues, but affect in the most tangible way the real rights of real people. In its infamous *Kelo* [*v. New London*] decision, the Supreme Court expanded the power of eminent domain beyond its constitutional limitation—public use—to the nebulous realm of public benefit. So "deference" to legislators and other government entities results in a free-for-all, with private property taken from citizen A and transferred to citizen B—precisely the danger against which the framers tried to protect us.

As with property, so too with traditional common-law liberties, such as the right to work in a lawful occupation. The hard lessons of judicial deference and abdication are taught, over and over again in this country.

An Example of Judicial Abdication

When Leroy Jones and his partners tried to establish a new taxicab company in Denver, they had everything they needed:

experience as drivers, untapped market demand, and capital; everything, that is, except a "certificate of public convenience and necessity" from the Colorado Public Utilities Commission. When they applied, they received the same response as every new taxicab applicant since World War II: application denied.

Mr. Jones challenged the power of this government commission to maintain a monopoly, but he came away empty-handed. Unfortunately, the "privileges or immunities" clause of the Constitution's 14th Amendment—designed precisely to protect freedom of enterprise from government interference—had been eviscerated more than a century ago in the Slaughterhouse Cases of 1873. (In these cases, the Supreme Court, by a 5-4 majority, upheld a state government monopoly of slaughterhouses in New Orleans that put scores of butchers out of business and nullified the constitutional protection of the clause.)

No thanks to the courts, at least in Mr. Jones's case, the media coverage shamed regulators into giving him a permit to establish a taxicab company.

What the Future Will Bring

Properly wielded, a court gavel can be David's hammer against the Goliath of big government. Among our governmental institutions, courts alone are designed to protect the individual against the tyranny of the majority—and against special interest groups with outsized influence.

The Rehnquist Court began to restrain unconstitutional exercise of government power in areas such as private property rights, equal protection, commerce and federalism that previous courts had allowed to run riot. But toward the end of the Rehnquist era its fervor began to subside. It remains to be seen whether the Roberts Court will proceed to boldly protect liberty, as the Constitution intended.

We all have a stake in seeing that it does, for as government inexorably expands, our freedom depends on the willingness of courts to rein in its excesses. For better or worse, the courts are the last line of defense against government running roughshod over individual liberty. When judges swear fealty to the Constitution, they must be mindful of the danger of exceeding the proper confines of judicial power, but as well the even greater danger of abdicating it.

> "Where judges usurp democratic legislative authority by imposing on the people their moral and political preferences under the guise of vindicating constitutional guarantees, they should be severely criticized and resolutely opposed."

U.S. Supreme Court Justices Should Not Practice Judicial Activism

Robert P. George

Robert P. George is a professor of jurisprudence and director of the James Madison Program at Princeton University in Princeton, New Jersey. The Family Research Council, for which this viewpoint was written, is a Christian organization that promotes the traditional family unit and traditional Christian values. In the following viewpoint, George traces the origins and major U.S. cases of what he views as judicial activism on the U.S. Supreme Court, such as the Dred Scott v. Sandford *and* Roe v. Wade *decisions. George argues that to minimize instances of*

Robert P. George, "Judicial Activism and the Threat to the U.S. Constitution," *Family Research Council*, 2005, pp. 1–14. Copyright © 2005 by the Family Research Council. All rights reserved. Reproduced by permission of Family Research Council, 801 G Street, NW, Washington, DC 20001, 1-800-225-4008, www.frc.org.

judges imposing their cultural and political ideology on U.S. society, Americans should work to ensure the nomination and confirmation of strict constitutionalist and originalist judges to the Supreme Court.

As you read, consider the following questions:

1. What did Thomas Jefferson predict with the decision in the *Marbury v. Madison* case?

2. Why does the author believe the *Dred Scott* case is a classic case of judicial activism?

3. What does the term "Lochnerizing" mean, according to the author?

Judicial power can be used, and has been used, for both good and ill. However, in a basically just democratic republic, judicial power should never be exercised—even for desirable ends—lawlessly. Judges are not legislators. The legitimacy of their decisions, particularly those decisions that overturn legislative judgments, depends entirely on the truth of the judicial claim that the court was authorized by law to settle the matter. Where this claim is false, a judicial edict is not redeemed by its good intentions or consequences. Decisions in which the courts usurp the authority of the people are not merely incorrect; they are themselves unconstitutional. And they are unjust.

Unfortunately, such decisions are growing in their number and the range of topics they cover. A crisis is at hand, and solutions must be found.

Should courts be granted the power to invalidate legislation in the name of the constitution? In reaction to Chief Justice John Marshall's opinion in the 1803 case of *Marbury v. Madison*,[1] Thomas Jefferson warned that judicial review would lead to a form of despotism.[2] Notably, the power of judicial review is nowhere mentioned in the Constitution. The courts themselves have claimed the power based on inferences drawn from the Constitution's identification of itself as supreme law, and the nature of the judicial office.[3] But even if we credit these inferences, as I am inclined to do, it must be said that early supporters of judicial review, including Marshall himself, did not imagine that the federal and state courts would claim the sweeping powers they exercise today. Jefferson and other critics were, it must be conceded, more far-seeing.

After *Marbury*, the power of the judiciary expanded massively. However, this expansion began slowly. Even if *Marbury* could be described as telling the Congress what it could and could not do, it would be another 54 years before the Supreme Court would do it again. And it could not have chosen a worse occasion. In 1857, Chief Justice Roger Taney handed down an opinion for the Court in the case of *Dred Scott v. Sandford*.[4] That opinion declared even free blacks to be noncitizens, and held that Congress was powerless to restrict slavery in the federal territories. It intensified the debate over slavery and dramatically increased the prospects for civil war.

Dred Scott was a classic case of judicial activism. With no constitutional warrant, the justices manufactured a right to hold property in slaves that the Constitution nowhere mentioned or could reasonably be read as implying. Of course, the Taney majority depicted their decision as a blow for constitutional rights and individual freedoms. They were protecting the minority (slaveholders) against the tyranny of a moralistic majority who would deprive them of their property rights. Of course, the reality was that the judges were exercising what in a later case would be called "raw judicial power"[5] to settle a debate over a divisive moral and social issue in the way they personally favored.

It took a civil war and several constitutional amendments (especially the 14th Amendment) made possible by the Union victory to reverse *Dred Scott v. Sandford*.

The *Dred Scott* decision is a horrible blight on the judicial record. We should remember, though, that while it stands as an example of judicial activism in defiance of the Constitution, it is also possible for judges to dishonor the Constitution by refusing to act on its requirements. In the 1896 case of *Plessy v. Ferguson*,[6] for example, legally sanctioned racial segregation was upheld by the Supreme Court despite the 14th Amendment's promise of equality. In *Plessy* the justices announced their infamous "separate but equal" doctrine, a doctrine that was a sham from the start. Separate facilities for blacks in the South were then, and had always been, inferior in quality. Indeed, the whole point of segregation was to embody and reinforce an ideology of white supremacy that was utterly incompatible with the principles of the Declaration of Independence and the 14th Amendment. Maintaining a regime of systematic inequality was the object of segregation. As Justice John Harlan wrote in dissent, segregation should have been declared unlawful because the Constitution of the United States is colorblind and recognizes no castes.[7]

A half century and more passed before the Supreme Court got around to correcting its error in *Plessy* in the 1954 case of *Brown v. Board of Education*.[8] In the meantime the Court repeated the errors that had brought it to shame in the *Dred Scott* case. The 1905 case of *Lochner v. New York*[9] concerned a New York law limiting to 60 the number of hours per week that the owner of a bakery could require or permit his employees to work. Industrial bakeries are tough places to work, even now. They were tougher—a lot tougher—then. Workers risked lung disease from breathing in the flour dust and severe burns from the hot ovens, especially when tired and less than fully alert. The New York state legislature sought to protect workers against abuse by limiting their working hours. But the Supreme Court said "no."

The justices struck down the law as an unconstitutional interference by the state in private contractual relations between employers and employees. The Court justified its action with a story similar to the one it told in *Dred Scott*. Again, it claimed to be protecting the minority (owners) against the tyranny of the democratic majority. It was restricting government to the sphere of public business, and getting it out of private relations between competent adults, namely, owners and workers.

The truth, of course, is that the Court was substituting its own laissez-faire economics philosophy for the contrary judgment of the people of New York acting through their elected representatives in the state legislature. On the controversial moral question of what constituted real freedom and what amounted to exploitation, unelected and democratically unaccountable judges, purporting to act in the name of the Constitution, simply seized decision-making power.[10] Under the pretext of preventing the majority from imposing its morality on the minority, the Court imposed its own morality on the people of New York and the nation.

Like *Dred Scott*, *Lochner* eventually fell, brought down not by civil war, but by an enormously popular president fighting a great depression. Under the pressure of Franklin Roosevelt's plan to pack the Supreme Court, the justices in 1937 repudiated the *Lochner* decision and got out of the business of blocking state and federal social welfare and worker protection legislation. Indeed, the term "Lochnerizing" was invented as a label for judicial rulings that overrode democratic law-making authority and imposed upon society the will of unelected judges.

For many years, the Court took great care to avoid the least appearance of Lochnerizing. In 1965, for example, in a case called *Griswold v. Connecticut*[11], the justices struck down a state law against contraceptives in the name of an unwritten "right to marital privacy." Justice William O. Douglas, who wrote the opinion, explicitly denied that he was appealing to the principle of *Lochner*.[12] Indeed, to avoid invoking *Lochner's* claim of a so-called "substantive due process" right in the 14th

Amendment, Douglas went so far as to say that he had discovered the right to privacy in "penumbras [rights guaranteed by implication in the Constitution] formed by emanations" of a panoply of Bill of Rights guarantees, including the Third Amendment's prohibition against the government quartering of soldiers in private homes in peacetime, and the Fourth Amendment's ban on unreasonable searches and seizures.

Griswold, though plainly judicial activism, was not an unpopular decision. The Connecticut statute it invalidated was rarely enforced and the public cared little about it. Its significance was mainly symbolic, and the debate about it was symbolic. The powerful forces favoring liberalization of sexual mores in the 1960s viewed the repeal of such laws—by whatever means necessary—as essential to discrediting traditional Judeo-Christian norms about the meaning of human sexuality. But the Court was careful to avoid justifying the invalidation of the law by appealing to sexual liberation or individual rights of any kind. In Douglas's account of the matter, it was not for the sake of "sexual freedom" that the justices were striking down the law, but rather to protect the honored and valued institution of marriage from damaging intrusions by the state. Otherwise uninformed readers of the opinion might be forgiven for inferring mistakenly that the ultraliberal William O. Douglas was in fact an archconservative on issues of marriage and the family. They would certainly have been justified in predicting—wrongly as it would turn out—that Douglas and those justices joining his opinion would never want to see the Griswold decision used to break down traditional sexual mores or encourage non-marital sexual conduct.

A mere seven years later, however, in *Eisenstadt v. Baird*,[13] the Court forgot everything it had said about marriage in the *Griswold* decision, and abruptly extended the "constitutional right" to use contraceptives to nonmarried persons. A year later, the justices, citing *Griswold* and *Eisenstadt*, handed down their decision legalizing abortion in *Roe v. Wade*. And the culture war began.

The *Roe* decision was pure Lochnerizing. *Roe* did for the cause of abortion what *Lochner* had done for laissez-faire economics and what *Dred Scott* had done for slavery. The justices intervened in a large scale moral debate over a divisive social issue, short circuiting the democratic process and imposing on the nation a resolution lacking any justification in the text or structure of the Constitution. Indeed, Justice Harry Blackmun, writing for the majority, abandoned *Griswold's* ideas of "penumbras formed by emanations" and grounded the new constitutional right to feticide in the Due Process Clause of the 14th Amendment, just where the *Lochner* court had claimed to discover a right to freedom of contract. Dissenting Justice Byron R. White accurately described the Court's abortion ruling as an "act of raw judicial power."

Having succeeded in establishing a national regime of abortion-on-demand by judicial fiat in *Roe*, the cultural left continued working through the courts to get its way on matters of social policy where there was significant popular resistance. Chief among these was the domain of sexual morality. Where state laws embodied norms associated with traditional Judeo-Christian beliefs about sex, marriage, and the family, left-wing activist groups brought litigation claiming that the laws violated 14th Amendment guarantees of due process and equal protection, and First Amendment prohibitions on laws respecting an establishment of religion. The key battleground became the issue of homosexual conduct. Initially, the question was whether it could be legally prohibited, as it long had been in the states. Eventually, the question became whether homosexual relationships and the sexual conduct on which such relationships are based must be accorded marital or quasi-marital status under state and federal law.

In 1986, the Supreme Court heard a challenge to Georgia's law forbidding sodomy in *Bowers v. Hardwick*.[14] Michael Hardwick had been observed engaging in an act of homosexual sodomy by a police officer who had lawfully entered

Hardwick's home to serve a summons in an unrelated matter. Left-wing activist groups treated Hardwick's case as a chance to invalidate sodomy laws by extending the logic of the Court's "right to privacy" decisions. This time, however, they failed. In a five-to-four decision written by Justice White, the Court upheld Georgia's sodomy statute as applied to homosexual sodomy. The justices declined to rule either way on the question of heterosexual sodomy, which the majority said was not before the Court.

The *Bowers* decision stood until 2003, when it was reversed in *Lawrence v. Texas*,[15] the case that set the stage for the current cultural and political showdown over the nature and definition of marriage. In *Lawrence*, the Court held that state laws forbidding homosexual sodomy lacked a rational basis and were invasions of the rights of consenting adults to engage in the type of sexual relations they preferred. Writing for the majority, Justice Anthony Kennedy claimed that such laws insult the dignity of homosexual persons. As such, he insisted, they are constitutionally invalid under the doctrine of privacy whose centerpiece was the *Roe* decision.

Kennedy went out of his way to say that the Court's ruling in *Lawrence* did not address the issue of same-sex marriage or whether the states and federal government were obliged to give official recognition to same-sex relationships or grant benefits to same-sex couples.[16] Writing in dissent, however, Justice Antonin Scalia said bluntly: "Do not believe it."[17] The *Lawrence* decision, Scalia warned, eliminated the structure of constitutional law under which it could be legitimate for lawmakers to recognize any meaningful distinctions between homosexual and heterosexual relationships.

On this point, many enthusiastic supporters of the *Lawrence* decision and the cause of same-sex "marriage" agreed with Scalia. They saw the decision as having implications far beyond the invalidation of anti-sodomy laws. Noting the sweep of Kennedy's opinion, despite his insistence that the justices

Defining Terms

If the terms "judicial activism" and "judicial restraint" have any meaning, it is that a court is activist when it is invalidating laws and overruling precedent, and restrained when deferring to popularly elected legislatures and following prior decisions.

Erwin Chemerinsky,
"Judicial Activism by Conservatives,"
Los Angeles Times, *June 27, 2008.*

were not addressing the marriage issue, they viewed the decision as a virtual invitation to press for the judicial invalidation of state laws that treat marriage as the union of a man and a woman. Indeed, litigation on this subject was already going forward in the states—it had begun in Hawaii in the early 1990s where a State Supreme Court ruling invalidating the Hawaii marriage laws was overturned by a state constitutional amendment. *Lawrence* turned out to be a new and powerful weapon to propel the movement forward and embolden state court judges to strike down laws treating marriage as the union of a man and a woman.

The boldest of the bold were four liberal Massachusetts Supreme Judicial Court justices who ruled in *Goodridge v. Massachusetts Department of Public Health*[18] that the Commonwealth's restriction of marriage to male-female unions violated the state constitution. The state legislature requested an advisory opinion from the justices about whether, a scheme of civil unions, similar to one adopted by the Vermont state legislature after a like ruling there would suffice. However, the four Massachusetts justices, over the dissents of three other justices said, "No, civil unions will not do."[19] And so same-sex marriage was imposed on the people of Massachusetts by un-elected and electorally unaccountable judges.

Clearly, the United States has endured episodes of judicial activism throughout its history. Just as clearly, incidents of judicial overreaching, much of it spurred by issues of sexual morality, are accelerating.

Here, there is a double wrong and a double loss, a crime with two victims. The first and obvious victim is the injured party in the case—the endangered worker, the unborn child, or the institution of marriage itself. The second is our system of deliberative democracy. In case after case, the judiciary is chipping away at the pillars of self-rule, undermining laws and practices, from statutes outlawing abortion to public displays of the Ten Commandments, that are deeply rooted in the American tradition.

Checking the "raw power" of today's judicial activists will require changes both in judicial personnel and targeted measures designed to remedy their specific abuses. For example, there is no alternative, in my judgment, to amending the Constitution of the United States to protect marriage. The Massachusetts state legislature has made an initial move towards amending the state constitution to overturn *Goodridge*, but the outcome is uncertain. The process of amending the Constitution of the Commonwealth of Massachusetts is lengthy and arduous (except, apparently, for the judges themselves). Even if the pro-marriage forces in Massachusetts ultimately succeed, liberal judges in other states are not far behind their colleagues on the Massachusetts bench. Hovering over the entire scene, like a sword of Damocles, is the Supreme Court of the United States which could, at any time, invalidate state marriage laws across the board. You may think: "They would never do that." Well, I would echo Justice Scalia: "Do not believe it." They would. And if they are not preempted by a *federal* constitutional amendment on marriage, they will. They will, that is, unless the state courts get there first, leaving to the U.S. Supreme Court only the mopping up job of invalidating the Defense of Marriage Act and requiring states to give "full faith and credit" to out-of-state same-sex "marriages."

My own view, however, is that we need a uniform national definition of marriage as the Union of one man and one woman. Here is why: Marriage is fundamental. Marriage is the basis of the family, and it is in healthy families that children are reared to be honorable people and good citizens. Marriage and the family are the basic units of society. No society can flourish when they are undermined. Until now, a social consensus regarding the basic definition of marriage meant that we didn't need to resolve the question at the federal level. Every state recognized marriage as the exclusive union of one man and one woman. (The federal government did its part at one point in our history to ensure that this would remain the case by making Utah's admission to the Union as a state conditional upon its banning polygamy.)

The breakdown of the consensus certainly does not eliminate the need for a uniform national definition. If we don't have one, then marriage will erode either quickly—by judicial imposition unless judges are stopped—or gradually by the integration into the formal and informal institutions of society of same-sex couples who, after all, possess legally valid marriage licenses from some state.[20] In the long run, it is untenable for large numbers of people to be considered married in one or some states of the United States yet unmarried in others. As Lincoln warned it would be with the evil of slavery in his time, it is inevitable that the country will go "all one way or all the other."

Slavery would either be abolished everywhere or it would spread everywhere. The same is true of same-sex "marriage," in the long run—and perhaps even in the not-so-long run.

Besides addressing specific examples of judicial activism, as the Federal Marriage Amendment would do, Americans can and should work to ensure the nomination and confirmation of constitutionalist judges to our courts, especially the Supreme Court.

If personnel on the Supreme Court do change, the question follows: is it legitimate for the Court to change its view of the law, and here, specifically, the Constitution? The legal doctrine of *stare decisis*—literally, to stand on what has been decided—is important and worthy of respect. That doctrine does not strictly bind, however, in cases in which a judicial decision is a gross misinterpretation of the Constitution, and especially where a decision constitutes a usurpation of the constitutional authority of the people to govern themselves through the institutions of deliberative democracy. The Supreme Court, over time, gradually backed away from its "freedom of contract" decisions and completely reversed itself in its decisions on racial segregation and the Jim Crow laws—and it was right to do so.

In *Planned Parenthood v. Casey*, the basic holding of *Roe* was reaffirmed by the Court on *stare decisis* grounds. Three of the justices who joined the majority—all Republican appointees—called on the "contending parties" in the debate over legal abortion to end their differences and accept the Court's ruling as a "common mandate rooted in the Constitution."

This was little more than a call for one side of the argument—the pro-life side—to surrender. Having written a series of abortion rulings lacking any basis in the Constitution, the justices took it upon themselves to ask the millions of Americans who oppose their unjustified ruling simply to submit to their ukase. Of course, the American people are under no obligation to "end their differences" by capitulating to judicial usurpation. On the contrary, they have every right under the Constitution to continue to oppose *Roe v. Wade* and work for its reversal. When judges exercising the power of judicial review permit themselves to be guided by the text, logic, structure, and original understanding of the Constitution, they deserve our respect and, indeed, our gratitude for playing their part to make constitutional republican government a reality. But where judges usurp democratic legislative authority by imposing on the people their moral and political preferences under the guise of vindicating constitutional guarantees, they should be severely criticized and resolutely opposed.

Notes

1. 5 U.S. (1 Cranch) 137 (1803).
2. See Thomas Jefferson's criticism of claims by the judiciary of authority to bind the other branches of government in matters of constitutional interpretation ("making the judiciary a despotic branch") in his Letter to Abigail Adams, September 11, 1804, in 11 WRITINGS OF THOMAS JEFFERSON (Albert E. Bergh ed. 1905), pp. 311-13.
3. See Marbury v. Madison.
4. 60 U.S. (19 How.) 393 (1856).
5. Roe v. Wade 410 U.S. 113, 222 (1973) (Justice Byron White, dissenting).
6. 163 U.S. 537 (1896).
7. Plessy v. Ferguson, 559 (Justice Harlan, dissenting).
8. 347 U.S. 483 (1954).
9. 198 U.S. 45 (1905).
10. See Lochner v. New York, 54-55 (Justice Holmes, dissenting). This is the standard reading of Lochner, shared by contemporary conservatives and liberals alike. For a powerful challenge to the standard reading, and a thoughtful defense of the majority opinion, see Hadley Arkes, "Lochner v. New York and the Cast of Our Laws," in Robert P. George (ed.), Great Cases in Constitutional Law (Princeton: Princeton University Press, 2000), ch. 5.
11. 381 U.S. 479 (1965).
12. See Griswold v. Connecticut, 482.
13. 405 U.S. 438 (1972).
14. 478 U.S. 186 (1986).

15. 123 S. Ct. 2472 (2003).

16. Lawrence v. Texas, 2484.

17. Lawrence v. Texas, 2498 (Justice Scalia, dissenting).

18. 798 N.E.2d 941 (Mass. 2003).

19. Opinion of the Justices to the Senate, 802 N.E.2d 565 (2003).

20. See Christopher Wolfe, "Why the Federal Marriage Amendment is Necessary," UNIVERSITY OF SAN DIEGO LAW REVIEW (forthcoming, 2005).

Periodical Bibliography

The following articles have been selected to supplement the diverse views presented in this chapter.

Jack M. Balkin   "Alive and Kicking," *Slate*, August 25, 2005. www.slate.com/id/2125226.

Radley Balko   "Supreme Court Ruling on Police Raids Endangers Citizens," *FoxNews.com*, June 21, 2006. www.foxnews.com/story/0,2933,200495,00.html.

Edward H. Crane   "The Key Issue for the Court Isn't Abortion," *Investor's Business Daily*, August 15, 2005.

Selwyn Duke   "Obama the Justifier," *American Thinker*, October 31, 2008. www.americanthinker.com/2008/10/obama_the_justifier.html.

Richard Epstein   "Trust Busters on the Supreme Court," *Wall Street Journal*, July 12, 2006.

Simon Lazarus   "More Polarizing Than Rehnquist," *The American Prospect*, May 14, 2007. www.prospect.org/cs/articles?article=more_polarizing_than_rehnquist.

Simon Lazarus and Harper Jean Tobin   "Justice Scalia's Two-Front War," *The American Prospect*, March 6, 2008. www.prospect.org/cs/articles?article=justice_scalias_two_front_war.

Robert A. Levy   "Judicial Appointments: What's on Tap from Obama and McCain?" *Findlaw*, October 2, 2008.

Thomas J. Miles and Cass R. Sunstein   "The Real Judicial Activists," *The American Prospect*, December 17, 2006. www.prospect.org/cs/articles?article=the_real_judicial_activists.

Bruce Shapiro   "Right-Wing Revelation," *Nation*, January 12, 2006. www.thenation.com/doc/20060130/shapiro.

For Further Discussion

Chapter 1

1. After reading the viewpoints by David von Drehle and Lisa L. Miller, do you believe the U.S. Supreme Court is an effective check on the executive branch? Explain your answer.

2. The treatment of suspected Taliban and al-Qaeda fighters has been a contentious issue. Read the viewpoints written by David D. Cole and Mark R. Levin. What is meant by the designation "enemy combatant" and what was the purpose of applying it to Guantanamo detainees? Do you think the fate of foreign prisoners should be a matter for judicial review? What should be the role of the U.S. Supreme Court in the process?

3. Is the Supreme Court an independent and impartial arbiter? Or is the Court infected by partisan politics that influence their decisions? Read the viewpoints of the Center for American Progress, Mark W. Smith, and Frederic F. Fleishauer to help flesh out your opinions on the issue.

Chapter 2

1. Should the U.S. Supreme Court uphold or reverse sodomy laws? Read viewpoints written by Robert Peters and Randy E. Barnett to bolster your opinions.

2. *Roe v. Wade* remains one of the most controversial U.S. Supreme Court decisions in history. James F. Pontuso offers a number of reasons *Roe* should be overturned by the Supreme Court. In another viewpoint, Cass Sunstein asserts the Court should let the decision stand. Read both viewpoints and present your opinion on the question.

3. Based on the viewpoints of Frederick S. Lane and Robert Bork, what do you perceive as the responsibility of the Supreme Court in deciding the role of religion in public life? Should issues of religion and public life be decided in the judicial system?

Chapter 3

1. The Center for American Progress argues that learning a Supreme Court nominee's political ideology should be a key function of the confirmation process. In a counter argument, Orrin Hatch contends there should not be a political litmus test for Supreme Court nominees. After reading both viewpoints, how do you view the confirmation process? Should a nominee's political ideology be relevant?

2. Should there be a religious litmus test for Supreme Court nominees? Read viewpoints by Annie Laurie Gaylor and Stephen B. Presser and Charles E. Rice to inform your answer.

3. In recent years, a number of legal scholars have debated the issue of implementing term limits on Supreme Court justices. After reading viewpoints written by Doug Bandow and Richard A. Posner, what is your opinion on the matter? What would be the benefits of term limits? What would be the drawbacks of term limits?

Chapter 4

1. Austen L. Parrish maintains that Supreme Court justices should feel free to use foreign court decisions when formulating their opinions on cases that come before them. Phyllis Schlafly contends the justices should refrain from relying on any foreign court decisions in their deliberations. After reading both viewpoints, do you think justices should be using foreign court decisions?

2. The debate of judicial activism has raged for the past several years. After reading viewpoints by Clint Bolick and Robert P. George, do you think Supreme Court justices should refrain from the practice of judicial activism? What is "judicial activism"? What are the benefits of judicial activism? What is the harm of practicing judicial activism?

Organizations to Contact

The editors have compiled the following list of organizations concerned with the issues debated in this book. The descriptions are derived from materials provided by the organizations. All have publications or information available for interested readers. The list was compiled on the date of publication of the present volume; the information provided here may change. Be aware that many organizations take several weeks or longer to respond to inquiries, so allow as much time as possible.

American Bar Association (ABA)
321 N Clark St., Chicago, IL   60654-7598
(312) 988-5000
e-mail: askaba@abanet.org
Web site: www.abanet.org

Comprised of more than 400,000 legal professionals, the American Bar Association is a voluntary organization that provides law school accreditation, continuing legal education, legal analysis and research, programs to assist lawyers and judges in their work, and initiatives to improve the legal system for the public. The ABA's Web site hosts a wide variety of blogs, including several that focus on the U.S. Supreme Court. They also publish the *ABA Journal*, a monthly magazine exploring a broad range of legal issues, and a variety of magazines, scholarly journals, and books. The ABA provides frequent analysis of U.S. Supreme Court decisions and other relevant legal issues.

American Civil Liberties Union (ACLU)
125 Broad St., 18th Fl., New York, NY   10004
(202) 393-4930 • fax: (757) 563-1655
Web site: www.aclu.org

The American Civil Liberties Union is a national organization that works to defend individual rights as guaranteed by the

U.S. Constitution. The ACLU, with over 500,000 members and supporters, works in the courts, communities, and legislatures to preserve civil liberties. The U.S. Supreme Court section of the ACLU Web site includes summaries of recent civil-rights–related cases heard by the Court as well as articles related to Court activities.

American Constitution Society for Law and Policy (ACS)
1333 H St. NW, 11th Fl., Washington, DC   20005
(202) 393-6181 • fax: (202) 393-6189
e-mail: info@ACSLaw.org
Web site: www.acslaw.org

ACS is a nonpartisan, nonprofit legal educational organization and network of lawyers, law students, scholars, judges, policy-makers, and individuals. ACS promotes the vitality of the U.S. Constitution and the fundamental values it expresses: individual rights and liberties, genuine equality, access to justice, democracy, and the rule of law. It hosts panel discussions to review U.S. Supreme Court decisions for its annual terms, and the society makes available on its Web site information about Court nominations and issue briefs that cover a range of legal topics, including Supreme Court decisions.

American Enterprise Institute for Public Policy Research (AEI)
115 17th St. NW, Washington, DC   20036
(202) 862-5800 • fax: (202) 862-7177
Web site: www.aei.org

The American Enterprise Institute for Public Policy Research was founded in 1943 as a private, nonprofit, libertarian, conservative institution to research matters of public policy and to educate the public on government, politics, economics, and social services. One of AEI's main activities is to sponsor research and conferences on topical matters. They also have a Web site that posts a number of publications, including commentaries, opinion-editorial articles, research papers, and their monthly newsletter, *AEI Newsletter*; videos and transcripts of its conferences; transcripts of government testimony of its scholars; and schedules of upcoming events. AEI has a publishing division, AEI Press, that has issued a range of books, including several studies of the U.S. Supreme Court.

Cato Institute

1000 Massachusetts Ave. NW, Washington, DC 20001-5403
(202) 842-0200 • fax: (202) 842-3490
Web site: www.cato.org

Founded in 1977, the Cato Institute is a nonprofit, conservative think tank that provides research and advocates for public policy proposals that support a conservative foreign and domestic agenda. Its main goal is to promote "the promise of political freedom and economic opportunity to those who are still denied it, in our own country and around the world." Cato publishes a number of resources on the U.S. Supreme Court, including the *Cato Supreme Court Review*, which compiles essays from leading conservative constitutional scholars on the most significant Supreme Court cases of the most recent term. Cato scholars also offer extensive analysis of and commentary on particular legal decisions and relevant Supreme Court issues, as well as a wide range of books on legal, political, and public policy issues.

Center for American Progress (CAP)

1333 H St. NW, 10th Fl., Washington, DC 20005
(202) 682-1611 • fax: (202) 682-1867
e-mail: progress@americanprogress.org
Web site: www.americanprogress.org

Founded in 2003, the Center for American Progress is a progressive think tank that researches, formulates, and advocates for a bold, progressive public policy agenda. Their aim is to restore the United States's global leadership; develop clean, alternative energies that support a sustainable environment; create economic growth and economic opportunities for all Americans; and advocate for universal health care. CAP scholars provide analyses of significant legal decisions and relevant

U.S. Supreme Court issues, as well as a wide range of books on legal, political, and public policy issues. The CAP Web site posts informational videos and video discussions, information on upcoming events, cartoons, interactive maps and quizzes, commentary on topical issues, and a listing of publications by CAP scholars.

Center for Constitutional Rights (CCR)
666 Broadway, 7th Fl., New York, NY   10012
(212) 614-6464
Web site: http://ccrjustice.org

Founded in 1966 by attorneys who represented civil rights activists in the South, CCR is a non-profit legal and educational organization dedicated to advancing and protecting the rights guaranteed by the U.S. Constitution and the Universal Declaration of Human Rights. CCR is dedicated to restoring the fundamental right to habeas corpus and has represented, as co-counsel, Guantanamo detainees in court, including before the U.S. Supreme Court.

Council on Foreign Relations (CFR)
1777 F St. NW, Washington, DC   20006
(202) 509-8400 • fax: (202) 509-8490
Web site: www.cfr.org

CFR is a nonpartisan and independent membership organization founded in 1921 that promotes understanding of foreign policy and the United State's role in the world. It convenes meetings at which government officials, global leaders, and CFR members debate major foreign-policy issues; by operating an international affairs think tank; by commissioning books and reports; and by publishing *Foreign Affairs*.

Federalist Society for Law and Public Policy Studies
1015 18th St. NW, Suite 425, Washington, DC   20036
(202) 822-8138 • fax: (202) 296-8061
e-mail: info@fed-soc.org
Web site: www.fed-soc.org

The Federalist Society is a group of more than 40,000 conservative and libertarian legal professionals who advocate for conservative principles. The organization is "founded on the principles that the state exists to preserve freedom, that the separation of governmental powers is central to the Constitution, and that it is emphatically the province and duty of the judiciary to say what the law is, not what it should be." The society's central aim is to sponsor fair, serious, and open debate about the need to enhance individual freedom and emphasize conservative and libertarian values in the U.S. legal system. They offer a number of resources, including a reading list for conservative undergraduate students, studies of the U.S. Supreme Court, and comprehensive analyses of state supreme courts.

Heritage Foundation
214 Massachusetts Ave. NE, Washington, DC   20002-4999
(202) 546-4400 • fax: (202) 546-8328
e-mail: info@heritage.org
Web site: www.heritage.org

Founded in 1973, the Heritage Foundation was established as a conservative think tank to "formulate and promote conservative public policies based on the principles of free enterprise, limited government, individual freedom, traditional American values, and a strong national defense." Heritage scholars research and formulate public policies to support these goals and then market them to lawmakers and the media in an attempt to shape public opinion on a number of key political, economic, and social issues that affect U.S. society in the twenty-first century. On its Web site can be found a bookstore featuring a range of books written by Heritage scholars. The Web site also posts commentary, lectures, government testimony by Heritage experts, press releases from the foundation, and listings of upcoming events.

Bibliography of Books

Vanessa A. Baird   *Answering the Call of the Court: How Justices and Litigants Set the Supreme Court Agenda*. Charlottesville, VA: University of Virginia Press, 2007.

Randy E. Barnett   *Restoring the Lost Constitution: The Presumption of Liberty*. Princeton, NJ: Princeton University Press, 2005.

Clint Bolick   *David's Hammer: The Case for an Activist Judiciary*. Washington, DC: Cato Institute, 2007.

Robert Bork, ed.   *A Country I Do Not Recognize: The Legal Assault on American Values*. Stanford, CA: Hoover Institution Press, Stanford University, 2006.

Erwin Chemerinsky   *Enhancing Government: Federalism for the 21st Century*. Stanford, CA: Stanford University Press, 2008.

Michael Comiskey   *Seeking Justices: The Judging of Supreme Court Nominees*. Lawrence, KS: University Press of Kansas, 2004.

Ronald Dworkin   *The Supreme Court Phalanx: The Court's New Right-Wing Bloc*. New York: New York Review Books, 2008.

Ronald B. Flowers   *That Godless Court?: Supreme Court Decisions on Church-State Relationships*. 2nd ed. Louisville, KY: Westminster John Knox Press, 2005.

Charles Fried

Saying What the Law Is: The Constitution in the Supreme Court. Cambridge, MA: Harvard University Press, 2004.

Kermit L. Hall and John J. Patrick

The Pursuit of Justice: Supreme Court Decisions That Shaped America. New York and Oxford: Oxford University Press, 2006.

Phillip E. Hammond, David W. Machacek, and Eric Michael Mazur

Religion on Trial: How Supreme Court Trends Threaten the Freedom of Conscience in America. Walnut Creek, CA: AltaMira Press, 2004.

Gary Hartman, Roy M. Mersky, and Cindy L. Tate

Landmark Supreme Court Cases: The Most Influential Decisions of the Supreme Court of the United States. New York: Facts on File, 2004.

Thomas M. Keck

The Most Activist Supreme Court in History: The Road to Modern Judicial Conservatism. Chicago: University of Chicago Press, 2004.

Michael J. Klarman

From Jim Crow to Civil Rights: The Supreme Court and the Struggle for Racial Equality. New York and Oxford: Oxford University Press, 2004.

Anthony A. Peacock

Deconstructing the Republic: Voting Rights, the Supreme Court, and the Founders' Republicanism Reconsidered. Washington, DC: AEI Press, 2008.

Stephen P. Powers
and Stanley
Rothman

*The Least Dangerous Branch?
Consequences of Judicial Activism.*
Westport, CT: Praeger, 2002.

Jamin B. Raskin

*Overruling Democracy: The Supreme
Court v. the American People.* New
York: Routledge, 2003.

Kermit Roosevelt

*The Myth of Judicial Activism:
Making Sense of Supreme Court
Decisions.* New Haven, CT: Yale
University Press, 2006.

Jeffrey Rosen

*The Most Democratic Branch: How
the Courts Serve America.* New York
and Oxford: Oxford University Press,
2006.

Suzanne U.
Samuels

*First Among Friends: Interest Groups,
the U.S. Supreme Court, and the Right
to Privacy.* Westport, CT: Praeger,
2004.

Herman Schwartz

*Right Wing Justice: The Conservative
Campaign to Take over the Courts.*
New York: Nation Books, 2004.

Jeffrey Toobin

*The Nine: Inside the Secret World of
the Supreme Court.* New York:
Anchor Books, 2007.

Mark V. Tushnet

*A Court Divided: The Rehnquist
Court and the Future of
Constitutional Law.* New York: W.W.
Norton Co., 2005.

Keith E.   Political Foundations of Judicial
Whittington   Supremacy: The Presidency, the
                        Supreme Court, and Constitutional
                        Leadership in U.S. History. Princeton,
                        NJ: Princeton University Press, 2007.

Christopher   That Eminent Tribunal: Judicial
Wolfe, ed.   Supremacy and the Constitution.
                        Princeton, NJ: Princeton University
                        Press, 2004.

Lawrence S.   The Psychology of the Supreme Court.
Wrightsman   New York and Oxford: Oxford
                        University Press, 2006.

Larry W. Yackle   Regulatory Rights: Supreme Court
                        Activism, the Public Interest, and the
                        Making of Constitutional Law.
                        Chicago: University of Chicago Press,
                        2007.

Index